THE AUTONOMOUS STATE OF CHILDCARE

For Huw

The Autonomous State of Childcare
Policy and the policy process in Britain

SERENA LIU
Anglia Polytechnic University

Ashgate

Aldershot • Burlington USA • Singapore • Sydney

Published by
Ashgate Publishing Limited
Gower House
Croft Road
Aldershot
Hampshire GU11 3HR
England

Ashgate Publishing Company
131 Main Street
Burlington, VT 05401-5600 USA

Ashgate website: http://www.ashgate.com

British Library Cataloguing in Publication Data
Liu, Serena
    The autonomous state of childcare : policy and the policy
    process in Britain
    1.Child care services - Government policy - Great Britain
    I.Title
    362.7'0941

Library of Congress Control Number: 00-110699

ISBN 0 7546 1570 7

Printed in Great Britain by
Antony Rowe Ltd, Chippenham, Wiltshire.

Contents

List of Figures

List of Tables

Preface

It was twenty years ago that I first wanted to write a book. Coming in and out of the imaginative world, I never dreamt that my first book would be an academic work on British policy and politics, using social theory.

This book comes from my Ph.D. thesis of a similar name, submitted to the Department of Sociology, University of Essex. Despite some 'crisis' periods during the course of doing this piece of work, it has unexpectedly aroused interest within close circles. Hopefully with publication, it will reach a wider audience, and be useful for other attempts to understand the social and political world.

The Ph.D. work was supervised mainly by Lydia Morris, and for some shorter periods, by Mary McIntosh and Rob Stones respectively. Further revision of the text benefited from the recommendations from John Scott, and Martin Smith of the University of Sheffield. The scholarship was refined by engaging with the many lectures, seminars and discussion groups of the Department of Sociology, University of Essex, during the three years when Anthony Woodiwiss was the Head of Department.

Grateful thanks are also sent to the Department of Sociology, University of Hong Kong, where I first studied sociology and gender; and to Good Hope School, Hong Kong, where I had the opportunity to learn English extensively.

The Rotary Foundation, Rotary International, funded the first year of my study in Britain. The Fuller/Bequest Research Fund of the Department of Sociology, University of Essex, supported the research expenses.

One of the greatest difficulties of doing this piece of work was to try to write English correctly. My partner, Huw James, has helped me all along. He has been very helpful and supportive in every way, without which this book would not be possible.

Serena Liu
Cambridge
July 2000

ix

List of Abbreviations

AGM	Annual General Meeting
AMA	Association of Metropolitan Authorities
BAECE	British Association for Early Childhood Education
CAVE	Campaign Against Vouchers in Education
CBC	Child Benefit Centre
CPS	Centre for Policy Studies
DES	Department of Education and Science
DFE	Department for Education
DfEE	Department for Education and Employment
DHSS	Department of Health and Social Security
DoH	Department of Health
ECEF	Early Childhood Education Forum
EYDCP	Early Years Development and Childcare Partnership
GM	Grant-Maintained
HC	House of Commons
HMSO	Her Majesty's Stationery Office
KCN	Kids' Clubs Network
LEA	Local Education Authority
LGMB	Local Government Management Board
LMS	Local Management Scheme
MP	Member of Parliament
NAHT	National Association of Head Teachers
NEYN	National Early Years Network
NCB	National Children's Bureau
NCMA	National Childminding Association
NCNE	National Campaign for Nursery Education
NUT	National Union of Teachers
NVC	Nursery Voucher Centre
NVQ	National Vocational Qualifications
Ofsted	Office for Standards in Education
PLA	Preschool Learning Alliance
PPA	Pre-school Playgroup Association
RgNI	Registered Nursery Inspector
SCAA	School Curriculum and Assessment Authority

SEN	Special Educational Needs
SSA	Standard Spending Assessment
TEC	Training and Enterprise Council
TES	Times Educational Supplement

1 Introduction

We make history, but history is not always made as we would wish. Public childcare provision in Britain is one of the issues that has raised much passion and been the source of much disappointment. Childcare provided by the public sector, which is free of charge to parents, has been limited. Public policy has been slow to change in terms of providing more childcare. Insufficient public childcare provision is an important barrier to the achievement of equal citizenship rights for women, in particular, the right to employment. Against this background, this book sets out to search for the crucial factors that have constrained the development of childcare policy and public childcare provision. It looks particularly at the developments in the 1990s which led to the introduction of the Nursery Education Voucher Scheme. This policy initiative was introduced by a Conservative Government in four pilot local authority areas in April 1996 and nationwide in April 1997. The original discussion which preceded the scheme started with the intention of expanding provision to improve employment opportunities for women. However the subsequent scheme, in only providing part-time pre-school education for four-year-olds, was of little help to women who wanted to take up paid work, but were bound by childcare commitments.

In this introductory chapter, I explain first the issue of childcare provision, its relation to women's rights to employment and other citizenship rights. Then, I present the analytical framework for the study. This is followed by an introduction to the Nursery Education Voucher Scheme and the process surrounding its conception, implementation and subsequent replacement. Last but not the least, I explain the research methods and the research process.

The Issue of Childcare Provision

Childcare provision refers to the provision of care and education for children below the age of compulsory schooling — those under five years-old in Britain. Public childcare provision refers specifically to childcare funded by public money — money raised from taxation. The key decisions for public provision are made by the central state apparatus in the form of public policy. However, historically the actual provision has been the responsibility of local authorities.

Although the definition of childcare involves aspects of both care and education, public childcare policy in Britain has considered the two as separate. On the issue of care (also known as 'daycare'), the policy has been to provide only for children who have special needs. In the case of other children, the responsibilities of arranging and financing care fall to the parents. On the issue of education (also known as 'nursery education' or 'pre-school education'), it has been the expressed desire of successive governments to provide part-time provision for all three- and four-year-olds whose parents want it. This differential approach to care and education is based on the belief that it is best for children under the age of two to be at home with their mothers. Only where special circumstances do not permit children to be cared for by their mothers should the public sector provide help. The provision of education for older children (three- and four-year-olds) is believed to be beneficial since children learn through activities with groups of other children. The provision, though, should remain part-time because young children should not be separated from their mothers for a whole day. This approach to childcare policy results in few publicly-funded places for daycare and many more places offering educational childcare. However, in either case there have never been enough places to cater for all three- and four-year-olds.

Publicly-funded daycare is usually made available through local authority maintained day nurseries. They offer full-time care all year round for children under five. In 1998 in England, there were 500 of these day nurseries providing care for 0.57 per cent of children aged under five (see Table 1.1). Publicly-funded pre-school education is usually provided by local education authority (LEA) maintained nursery schools, nursery classes and reception classes in schools. The various settings supply different levels of provision. Nursery schools provide half day sessions during term time. Nursery classes offer a similar provision to that of nursery schools. They differ from nursery schools in that they are part of schools and do not have separate premises and headteachers. Reception classes are also part of schools. They involve more structured teaching similar to that received by children of compulsory education age. Children have to work within a timetable, usually from 9 a.m. to 3:15 p.m. in term time. In 1998 in England, nursery schools and classes in total were catering for 27.77 per cent of three- and four-year-olds while reception classes were providing for 26.55 per cent (see Table 1.1).

Public provision may also exist in the form of family centres. They offer a range of services to children and their families. They are usually attended by one or more of the parents with their children, often on a 'drop in' basis. There were 490 family centres in England in 1998, although a small proportion of them were privately-owned.[1]

Table 1.1 The Levels of Childcare Provision in England, 1998

Premises	Categories	Number of premises	Number of places	Percentage of provision
Day nurseries	Public	500	18,670	0.57[a]
	Independent	6,100	203,000	6.25[a]
Childminders	Independent	94,700	370,700	11.41[a]
Playgroups	Independent	15,700	383,600	28.92[a]
Nursery schools	Full-time	533	8,247	27.77[b]
	Part-time		40,389	
Nursery classes	Full-time	6,015	30,662	
	Part-time		289,060	
Reception classes	Full-time	--	321,122	26.55[b]
	Part-time		30,99	
Independent schools	Independent	--	52,252	3.94[b]

[a] Percentage of 0-4 year-olds.
[b] Percentage of 3-4 year-olds.

Source: Early Childhood Unit, National Children's Bureau (NCB), compiled from government statistics.

The level of public childcare provision varies significantly across regions. It is the responsibility of local authorities to make the actual provision, but they are only required by law to provide daycare for children who are 'in need'. Other provision is dependent on an individual council's policy. Some councils are keen to provide the service but some are not. In March 1998 in England, the number of publicly-funded day nurseries varied from 0 in forty-nine local authorities, to 202 in Birmingham. The number of places offered by these local councils varied from 0 to more than 7,700.[2] In January 1998, the percentage of three- and four-year-olds in

LEA-maintained educational provision varied from 27 per cent in Leicestershire, to 100 per cent in Hartlepool, Redcar and Cleveland, and Stockton-on-Tees.[3]

The insufficient childcare provision in the public sector has not been able to meet the demand for childcare facilities. This has triggered a significant and continual development of the independent sector. Major forms of independent provision include private nurseries, childminding and pre-schools (playgroups). There are also independent schools and nannies.

Private nurseries offer a full-time service for children under five, usually all year round. The provision may involve educational elements for three- and four-year-olds. They may be run by community groups, commercial companies, or employers for their employees in the workplaces. In 1998 in England, there were 6,100 registered private nurseries providing for 6.25 per cent of children aged under five (Table 1.1).

Childminders look after children aged 0-7 in the childminders' own home. Terms and fees are arranged privately with parents. Childminding experienced significant development in the 1960s and 1970s. The number of childminders continued to grow in the 1980s and 1990s. In 1998 in England, there were 94,700 registered childminders, offering places equivalent to 11.41 per cent of the total number of children aged 0-4 (Table 1.1). However, it should be noted that since childminders provide for children aged 0-7 and there were no separate figures indicating the number of childminding places for under-fives, the actual percentage of under-fives with childminders should be less than the figure presented.

Pre-schools/playgroups usually offer half-day sessions, not necessarily every day of the week. They may be run by local communities or voluntary groups and are referred to as the voluntary sector. They are usually free or are provided at low cost to parents. The earliest playgroups were established in the 1960s by mothers who recognized the need for their children to play in the company of other children. Since there were no publicly-funded nursery places available for them, they started groups of their own.[4] Playgroups gradually developed to emphasize the educational purpose of the provision and changed name to pre-schools at the beginning of the 1990s. In 1998 in England, there were 15,700 pre-schools providing places equivalent to 28.92 per cent of the total number of three- and four-year-olds.[5]

Some independent schools offer educational childcare for children aged three and four. They were providing for 3.94 per cent of children in this age range in 1998 in England. Also within the category of independent provision are nannies. They are privately employed by parents to look after children in the family home. Nannies are exempt from registration if they look after the children of one or two families. There are no figures available concerning the number of nannies and the number of children they look after.

The provision in the independent sector has helped to supplement the insufficient childcare facilities provided by the public sector. However, there are problems associated with independent provision. The majority of independent providers charge fees for their services. It was suggested that the typical cost of childcare for a family with two children, one under-five and one at school, was 6,000 pounds a year in 1999, more than the average family spending on food or housing.[6] Low income families are unlikely to be able to afford independent provision, or may only be able to afford part-time provision. In addition, there is usually no coordination with regard to the distribution and development of independent providers. There may not be any providers in some areas and there may be insufficient in some others.

Both public and independent provision together are not enough to cater for all children under-five. In particular, as much of the provision (especially that orientated towards educational childcare) is part-time, many children are using more than one kind of service. Hence, in 1998, the percentage of children being provided for should be less than the sum of the figures presented. Those children who are not provided with a publicly-funded place or only have it part-time, if their parents cannot afford independent provision or can only afford it part-time, or if there is no provision accessible to them, they have to be looked after by relatives or parents, usually mothers.

The sociological significance of the issue is that childcare responsibility is an important barrier to the achievement of equal citizenship rights for women. Citizenship is a contested concept describing the basic rights and obligations of individuals as members of a community. In reality, citizenship rights and obligations are defined by law or public policy through the policy making process of a political state. In the realm of social studies, the best known modern conception of citizenship rights is that by T. H. Marshall. He identifies three elements to citizenship rights — civil, political and social:

> The civil element is composed of the rights necessary for individual freedom — liberty of the person, freedom of speech, thought and faith, the right to own property and to conclude valid contacts, and the right to justice ... By the political element I mean the right to participate in the exercise of political power, as a member of a body invested with political authority or an elector of the members of such a body ... By the social element I mean the whole range from the right to a modicum of economic welfare and security to the right to share to the full in the social heritage and to live the life of a civilized being

according to the standards prevailing in the society (Marshall, 1964, pp. 71-72).

Based on Marshall's definition of citizenship rights, childcare responsibilities most directly affect the achievement of the social aspect of the citizenship rights of women. It also hinders the fulfilment of their political citizenship rights.

A woman with childcare responsibilities is less of a citizen in terms of her social rights to economic welfare by wage-earning through paid work. Such a woman is in an inferior position in the labour market. The presence of dependent children in the family has been found to be the major reason contributing to women's lower rate of economic activity and employment. According to the Labour Force Survey,[7] in spring 1998, 72 per cent of women of working age (16-59) were economically active,[8] compared with 84 per cent of men (16-64). Of those women with children aged under five, only 55 per cent were economically active; for those whose youngest child was aged 5-10, the rate increased to 72 per cent; and for those with the youngest child aged 11-15, the rate increased to 78 per cent. A similar pattern was found in the rate of employment.[9] 68 per cent of all women of working age were in employment, compared with 78 per cent of men. The employment rates of women with dependent children increased from 50 per cent for those whose youngest child was under 5, to 68 per cent for those whose youngest child was aged 5-10, to 74 per cent for those whose youngest child was 11-15. A comparison of the effect of gender and childcare on the rate of economic activity and employment is presented in table 1.2.

Women with dependent children are more likely to experience part-time and intermittent employment. In the same Labour Force Survey, a much higher proportion of women who were in employment worked part-time, especially those with childcare responsibilities. 44 per cent of women in employment worked part-time compared with 8 per cent of men. 60 per cent of employed women with dependent children (under 16) worked part-time, compared with 32 per cent of those without dependent children. Women with younger children (aged 0-10) were more likely to work part-time than those with older children (aged 11-15): 65 per cent compared with 52 per cent. Women also tended to stay with their employer for a shorter time than men, especially those women with dependent children. 36 per cent of men had been with their current employer for over 10 years, compared with 23 per cent of women with dependent children and 28 per cent of women without dependent children. Conversely, 30 per cent of men and 35 per cent of women had been with their current employer for less than two years. The proportion increased to 38 per cent for women

Table 1.2 The Effect of Gender and Childcare on Economic Activity and Employment

	Economic activity (Percentage)	Employment (Percentage)
Men	84	78
Women	72	68
with youngest child aged 0-4	55	50
with youngest child aged 5-10	72	68
with youngest child aged 11-15	78	74

Source: Labour Force Survey, Spring 1998, in *Labour Market Trends*, March 1999.

with children aged 1-10. Both intermittent and part-time employment are associated with lower career prospects and lower pay. In April 1997, the average hourly rate for women in full-time employment was 7.88 pounds.[10] This represented 80 per cent of the average rate for men at 9.82 pounds per hour. The part-time rate was 5.77 pounds per hour for women. This represented 84 per cent of the rate for men at 6.90 pounds per hour.

A woman who is in an inferior position in the labour market is also less of a citizen in terms of entitlement to welfare benefits from the welfare system. The right of an individual to welfare benefits is linked to their position in the labour market. As noted by Pateman, welfare provision has been established through a 'two-tier system' (1989, p. 188). The first tier involves social security benefits such as unemployment subsidies, insurance and pension. These are benefits available to individuals as public persons by virtue of their participation in the labour market. The entitlement to these benefits depends on previous employment status and National Insurance contributions. Women who have no paid work are excluded by such a system. Women who have low paid work are disadvantaged by it. The second tier of welfare provision involves non-contributory social security benefits. These are benefits available to the dependents of the first category, when the latter can not support them, or to other private individuals. Women who have no paid work due to childcare responsibilities and are the dependent of the male breadwinner are in this category. This second tier of welfare provision is intended to fill some gaps left by the first tier. However, the non-contributory benefits are deliberately maintained at a lower level than the contributory ones, so that they do not undermine the contributory principle of the welfare system (see Lister, 1993). Therefore, as long as childcare provided for one's own children from within the private family remains unpaid and is not recognized in the same way as paid work by the welfare state, women with childcare responsibilities are deprived of the social right to economic welfare and security.

A woman with childcare responsibilities is also less of a citizen in terms of the right to political participation. Lack of time and lack of money are the major constraints (see Ibid.). Political participation takes time, but looking after children is usually a 24-hour task and is combined with other household responsibilities. Those women with childcare responsibilities simply would not have the time to get involved in politics. Political participation also requires mobility and money. Women with dependent children who are not in paid work or have low paid jobs would be unlikely to have the necessary financial resources. However, political participation is important for the pursuit of social welfare rights. As argued by Dietz, 'the pursuit of those social and economic concerns must be undertaken through active engagement as citizens in the public world' (1992, p. 453). Insufficient participation in the political sphere by women only furthers their inferior position in the labour market and welfare system.

Public childcare provision is important in aiding the achievement of equal social and political citizenship rights for women. Some may argue that women may prefer to work part-time or not at all, but would prefer to look after children.[11] However, for other women with young children who would like to work and would like to participate more in public life, they are deprived of the opportunity, partly and importantly, by the limited public childcare provision. Reflecting the important role that public childcare provision plays, this study sets out to explore the crucial factors that have influenced the development of childcare policy and public childcare provision. Consequently, it will shed light on the elements that have constrained the attainment of equal citizenship rights for women.

The Analytical Schema

Why is policy slow to change in terms of providing more public childcare? There has been some reviving of interest in this issue among academics in recent years. Such interest, however, is limited and varies in the approach to the problem. Marchbank (1996) explains why childcare was the only issue which failed to achieve national agenda status and national legislation from among the original Four Demands of the British Women's Liberation Movement.[12] She examines the nature of pressure politics on women's interest issues, methods of organizing public and private debates and women's attitudes to the childcare issue. She argues that 'the more successful feminist issues do not challenge gender roles to the same extent as childcare does', which explains the 'nonmobilization of childcare as an issue' (p. 9). By focusing on the pressure politics of civil society, Marchbank's analysis includes the pluralist assumption that policy making is the result of interest representation and pressure. Little attention is paid to the role of political institutions and the extent to which they are able to influence policy making.

Successive works of Randall (1995, 1996) present a historic and political analysis of why there is insufficient public provision for childcare. Her work is concerned with both political institutions and pressure groups. She analyses the instances where childcare has been brought to the attention of politicians or interest groups. The reasons she identifies are mainly organisational (e.g. fragmentation of responsibility between central departments and between central and local governments) and ideological (e.g. the ideology of motherhood). There is no systematic analysis of the process of policy making. No account is given of the structure of policy making, i.e. the nature of the relationships among political institutions and interest groups, and the effect of these structural factors on policy outcomes.

For a better understanding of the issue in question, I consider it necessary to carry out a systematic analysis of the policy process of childcare policy. I define 'policy' in its broad sense as consisting of a course of actions or a web of decisions[13] by policy actors. The 'policy process' is the dynamic process in which such actions and decisions are produced. Hence, the analysis of the policy process has two dimensions — the 'actors' and the dynamic 'process' itself (Figure 1.1). Analysis along the dimension of 'actors' is concerned with three questions. Firstly, who are the policy actors? Secondly, what are their actions and decisions? Thirdly, why do they undertake such actions and make these decisions? 'Policy actors' is used here to refer to individual actors, political institutions and private organizations (a collective of individual actors), who have participated in the policy process and have sought to influence policy decision making.

Inspired by Giddens's theory of structuration, I consider there are three aspects to understanding why actors undertake certain actions and decisions. First of all, previous actions and decisions and their consequences have an effect on later actions and decisions. Giddens (1984) conceives action as being in a continuous flow. The consequences of a previous action feed back to become the unacknowledged conditions of later action. Thus, an action continued to influence future actions.

Secondly, actors draw upon 'rules' for their actions and decisions. 'Rules' are usually not overtly formulated and written, but situated in actors' heads. Just like mathematical formulae which 'programme' a sequence of numbers, rules 'programme' the activities of the human agent. I regard the 'rules' that are involved in the policy process to be the values, beliefs, ideologies and interests of actors which influence their actions and decisions. Finally, actors' actions and decisions are affected by their resources. It is from these resources that relationships of resource dependency are formed between actors. Those actors who have control over the most crucial resources, upon which other actors are most heavily dependent, are the most powerful and influential in policy making. The policy options they prefer are most likely to become policy. The rules they draw upon are most likely to influence policy. This aspect of resource relationships between policy actors is the most important in understanding policy outcomes.

The dynamic 'process' is another dimension in the analysis of the policy process. This 'process' starts when an issue gains the attention of

---

Dimension 1   Actors*

    Question 1   Who are the policy actors?
    Question 2   What are their actions and decisions?
    Question 3   Why do they make such decisions and take such
                actions?
        Aspect 1   Previous actions and decisions (previous policy)
        Aspect 2   Rules (values, beliefs, ideologies and interests)
        Aspect 3   Resources (relationships of resource dependency and
                 power)

Dimension 2   Process

    Stage 1 (agenda setting) → Stage 2 → Stage 3 → ... → Stage n (policy termination or succession)

---

*Dimension 1 varies along dimension 2.

Figure 1.1 Policy Process Analysis

policy actors and is put onto the policy agenda. It continues when a policy initiative is formulated to tackle the issue, and when the policy initiative is implemented. The process ends when the policy initiative is terminated or succeeded. Thus, the policy process can be seen as separated into some distinct but highly related stages, such as agenda setting, policy formulation, implementation and termination.[14] Each of the stages serves a different function in the policy process and has different implications for policy outcomes. There may be different policy actors involved at each stage. The role and influence of an actor may be different in different stages. Each of the policy stages requires an independent and detailed analysis.

The framework for the analysis of the policy process described above will be discussed in more detail in chapter 2. Through the analysis, the deciding factors which have influenced policy making should be made apparent. I would also like to consider the relevance of existing theoretical traditions on the state to childcare policy making. These theoretical traditions include pluralism, Marxism and state autonomy.

There is no single theory of Marxism.[15] A characteristic stance is that the interests of the capitalist class or the system of capitalist production is the most important in influencing state action and policy making. Two strands of contemporary Marxist thinking can be distinguished — instrumentalist Marxism and structuralist Marxism. Structuralist Marxism as advocated by Poulantzas (1973) argues that the state works to protect the long-term framework of capitalist production and to ensure the conditions for capital accumulation. For this purpose the state may be in conflict with some fractions of the capitalist class and so it has to be relatively autonomous from the influence of the capitalists. In instrumentalist Marxism as advocated by Miliband (1969), the state acts on behalf of the ruling capitalist class and protects the latter's interests. The state is the instrument for bourgeois domination. This role of the state arises not only from the capitalist system of production, but also from the similar social background of the state elite and the capitalist class.

There is also no single theory of pluralism.[16] A characteristic stance of the pluralist view is that interest groups are important in influencing state action and policy making. Society is composed of diverse and fragmented interests. People with shared interests come together voluntarily or organizationally to form groups in order to assert their social identity and political demands. Some groups, such as business, are more resourceful and powerful than others. However, the existence of many groups ensures that there are multiple power centres and no one group is dominant. The conventional pluralist view considers that the state is the arbitrator who seeks to balance competing interests and demands. A revisionist view, however, argues that states and governments are important interest groups themselves.

Advocates of state autonomy grant the state the 'explanatory centrality' in policy making (Skocpol, 1985, p. 6). This is because states have the potential for autonomous action. They have goals of their own and have the capacity to act in accordance with their goals (Skocpol, 1985). They are able to translate their own policy preferences into policy, despite the preferences of other actors (Nordlinger, 1981). In other words, states can act autonomously in policy making, neither constrained by the capitalist or economic interest, nor the requests or demands from other interest groups in society. In view of this, it is necessary to bring 'the state back in to a central place in analysis of policy making' (Skocpol, 1985, p. 20).

When speaking of state autonomy, some commentators have drawn attention to the fact that the state is not a unified entity. It is nothing but 'a distinct set of political institutions that have the authority to make the rules that govern society' (Smith, 1993, p. 2). In Britain these institutions include the Government, government departments, the Civil Service, Parliament, local councils, etc. Actors occupying different positions in different political institutions have different roles in the political system. They may share a common goal, but they may have distinctive or even conflicting goals and formulate different policy preferences. Therefore, it is unlikely that all state actors have autonomy, or have the same level of autonomy, in policy making. The notion of 'state autonomy' is more suitably seen as shorthand for certain state actors having autonomy in policy making with respect to other state actors and actors in society. The discussion needs to clarify which state actors have the autonomy, and in relation to whom. The notion of state autonomy and the explanatory concepts for its understanding will be explored further in chapter 2.

The study of childcare policy and the policy process in the following chapters, reveals that the theoretical stance of state autonomy is more relevant to the reality of childcare policy making than either Marxism or pluralism. However, the empirical situation is more complicated than that indicated by the notion of state autonomy in its simplest form. The Marxist and pluralist view points are not entirely irrelevant. Who the most influential actors are, the form and the degree of their influence, varies in different stages of the policy process. The relevance of the different theories of the state to the empirical situation will be discussed in full in subsequent chapters.

The Nursery Education Voucher Scheme

The analysis in this book focuses on the developments in the 1990s which led to the introduction of the Nursery Education Voucher Scheme. This policy initiative was piloted in four local authorities from April 1996 and implemented nationwide in April 1997. Parents of every four-year-old were given a voucher of 1,100 pounds to exchange for a year of pre-school education. The provision was mainly part-time (except some reception classes which were full-time) — 2.5 hours a session for 5 sessions a week, during term time and for three terms a year. It could be made by institutions in the public, private or voluntary sectors. The reason for choosing this particular policy initiative is that it involved the largest ever amount of public money allocated for the childcare sector at that time. The discussion leading to the policy initiative started with the intention of expanding public childcare provision in order to aid women's employment prospects. However, the resulting voucher scheme only aimed to provide part-time pre-school education for four-year-olds. A provision of this form offered little help for women who wanted to take up employment but were bound by childcare. The voucher scheme was conceived largely according to the policy preferences of a few central state actors — the leading members of the government. It diverged by a large extent from the preferences of major interest groups in society and actors at the periphery of the state (e.g. local authorities). The policy initiative was terminated after only one term of nationwide operation by the newly-elected Labour Government following the May 1997 General Election.

It is inadequate to consider the voucher scheme as an isolated case of its own. The policy initiative is simply situated at one point in the history of childcare policy and is influenced by prior policies. As mentioned earlier in the discussion, one of the aspects to understanding why actors undertake certain actions and decisions (policy making), is the effect of previous actions and decisions (previous policy). Therefore, understanding the policies prior to the voucher scheme and their effect on childcare provision is necessary for a proper understanding of the emergence of the policy initiative. Chapter 3 is devoted to a review of childcare policy and childcare provision in history, from its earliest days to the present time. Its purpose is to identify the issues that were to influence the form of the voucher scheme, and to demonstrate the continuous significance of these issues in the further development of childcare policy and provision. The chapter is also valuable in providing a historical overview of the development of childcare policy and childcare provision.

The policy process of the voucher scheme is considered in six stages: 'agenda setting', 'option selection', 'legislation', 'policy negotiation', 'implementation' and 'replacement'. 'Agenda setting' refers to the stage which culminated in the provision of pre-school education for four-year-olds reaching the government's policy agenda. The inclusion of younger children and the provision of any element of care were discounted. The then Prime Minister John Major made a 'cast iron' commitment to the chosen form of provision at the Conservative Party Conference in October 1994. 'Option selection' is the stage at which the Government selected a universal voucher scheme, from other options, as a way of achieving the Prime Minister's promise. The Secretary of State for Education and Employment announced this decision in the House of Commons on 6 July 1995. 'Legislation' is the stage at which the legislation required for the nationwide implementation of the voucher scheme went through Parliament. It was introduced to Parliament in January 1996 and in July 1996 the Nursery Education and Grant-Maintained Schools Bill received the Royal Assent. 'Policy negotiation' refers to the stage at which the Department for Education and Employment (DfEE), on behalf of the Government, carried out negotiations with interest organizations and local authorities concerning arrangements under the voucher scheme and participation in Phase One — the pilot scheme. 'Implementation' refers to the stage of implementing the vouchers in Phase One areas from April 1996 and nationwide in April 1997. 'Replacement' is the stage at which the Labour Government replaced the voucher scheme soon after its election victory in May 1997.

Chapter 4 looks at the first three policy stages of 'agenda setting', 'option selection' and 'legislation'. There was a significant increase in the demand for childcare facilities in the 1980s. There was also heightened political pressure from society for more public childcare provision. The Conservative Government was not able to ignore the issue any longer. The Ministerial Group on Women's Issues suggested the provision of full-time childcare for children under-five, whose mothers went out to work, through tax-free vouchers supplied by employers. The proposal was opposed by some actors at the centre of the state, including the Prime Minister, ministers from the Treasury Office and other right-wing ministers. They instead preferred the provision of pre-school education, which was historically part-time, for four-year-olds. One of their 'rules' was to minimise public expenditure, and provision of this kind of pre-school education would be cheaper. Limiting provision in this way also addressed another of their 'rules' that mothers ought to stay at home to bolster the family, and public policy should not encourage mothers of young children to go out to work. These leading members of the government had the centralized resources which were necessary for any expansion in childcare provision. They acted autonomously and put the provision of pre-school education for four-year-olds onto the policy agenda, in accordance with their own policy preference.

The question then was, how best to make the provision? Right-wing ministers preferred a universal voucher scheme, drawing upon their 'rule' to create markets for the provision of public services. They thought that by giving parents of every eligible child vouchers to 'purchase' pre-school education, the policy initiative would create a competitive market for under-fives provision. Ministers from the Treasury Office, drawing upon their rule of minimising public expenditure, preferred the cheaper universal voucher system. The Prime Minister, mindful of election victory, also favoured the universal voucher scheme. He considered that giving parents of every four-year-old a voucher would prove to be a vote-winner. Ministers and civil servants from the Department for Education (DFE), the government department responsible for pre-school education, originally opposed the voucher option. They argued that a voucher scheme would not be the best way to expand provision because no money would be available specifically for the creation of new places. They favoured a bidding system under which providers would bid for funding for expanding provision. Local authorities, childcare and education interest groups also opposed the voucher option for similar reasons. However, the leading members of the government who supported vouchers had the centralized resources which were necessary for any policy development. They exercised power over ministers and civil servants from the DFE who eventually agreed to a universal voucher scheme.

Legislation was required to create a legal basis for the voucher scheme to be implemented nationwide. Ministers united to press their policy proposal through Parliament, despite previous disagreement. A majority of the Conservative Members of Parliament (MPs) supported the Government but a handful did not. The latter considered that some arrangements under the Government's proposal would not be beneficial to the society groups they represented or had close contact with. Opposition MPs protested against the proposal because it would not lead to an expansion in provision. A majority of the Peers in the House of Lords disagreed with the proposal for a similar reason. Despite various opposing voices, the Government successfully pressed the legislation through Parliament. The central state actors had the crucial resources for making legislation which gave them power over other state actors in Parliament and gave them autonomy in legislating.

Chapter 5 is concerned with the stage of 'policy negotiation'. Once the decision for a voucher scheme was made at the centre of the state machinery, it was up to the government department responsible to press it through and carry it out. Ministers and civil servants from the DfEE[17] undertook negotiations with interest groups and local authorities. There were four major incidents during this stage. Firstly, the Pre-school Learning Alliance (PLA) represented their member pre-schools, who were initially given a half-rate voucher, to demand a full-rate one. Secondly, the National Childminding Association (NCMA) represented their member childminders, who were excluded from participating in the voucher scheme, to campaign for inclusion. Thirdly, local authorities volunteered to try out the vouchers in Phase One — the pilot scheme. Fourthly, the Government carried out consultations on the 'quality assurance regime' and the 'desirable outcomes for children's learning' of the voucher scheme. Apart from these four major incidents, there were a number of national or local campaigns against the voucher scheme organized by national or local campaigning groups. The Audit Commission, the government's official watch-dog, also expressed its concern over the possible adverse effects of the policy initiative on pre-school education provision.

Although this policy stage featured a high degree of participation by interested actors, the majority of them had no influence upon policy decisions. Only pre-schools and local authorities, who had some crucial resources that the Government needed for implementing the voucher scheme, were able to influence some policy decisions, but not those affecting the core components.

Chapter 6 looks at the policy stages of 'implementation' and 'replacement'. The voucher scheme was first piloted in four local authority areas in Phase One, then nationwide a year later in Phase Two. The scheme involved a complicated mechanism of nine stages which caused confusion among parents and brought an extra work burden for providers. Despite the apparent problems, the resources of the government ensured the relatively smooth running of the implementation stage. However, implementation was unsuccessful in achieving the aims of the voucher scheme: to expand provision; to enhance parental choice; to ensure the quality of provision; to encourage the development of the private and voluntary sectors, and hence to create a free market for pre-school education provision. Ministers had no control over providers of pre-school education who were crucial for implementing the vouchers, and thus had no control over the outcome of implementation. One month after Phase Two began, the Conservative Party lost power in the 1997 General Election. The new Labour Government soon replaced the voucher scheme in accordance with their preferred plan.

The concluding chapter summarizes the factors which influenced the formulation of the voucher scheme. The voucher scheme was, to a large extent, the result of the leading members of the government having a high degree of autonomy in policy making. However, the result of their autonomous action was to fail to achieve the aims of the policy initiative and to miss the opportunity to expand pre-school education provision. Most importantly, the opportunity to develop the form of childcare provision which would assist women with paid work participation was lost. In view of this, the book concludes by suggesting measures that would lead to policy making being more responsive to social demand, and in this case, to the provision of more public childcare. This includes a rethinking of state autonomy, its implication for representative democracy, and the future of governance.

The above is a brief summary of some of the major issues. It is necessary to read each individual chapter in order to appreciate the essence of the substantive arguments.

Research Methods and the Research Process

Empirical data used in the discussion were gathered from a vast amount of documents and some semi-structured interviews. I started the research by searching libraries for published material concerning childcare. I was able to find some secondary work by academics and some published material by private organizations and state institutions interested in childcare. However, this material was limited and did not concentrate on any specific policy initiative. Nevertheless, they provided me with a primary understanding of the childcare issue. They also helped me to identify the major interest groups in the childcare sector.

I sent letters to about ten of these interest groups in February 1997 to ask for interviews. Most of the groups responded by sending me their publications including periodic magazines, newsletters, and annual reports. I believe this kind of response was due to the fact that I did not address the letters to persons in positions of responsibility. It was likely that the letters had been left to people who were not in a position to make a decision to see me, but did their best by sending me publications. I was granted an interview by two interest groups — the Kids' Clubs Network (KCN) and the NCB, and paid a visit to one other — the Daycare Trust. Through the meeting with the Chief Executive of KCN, I got to know the organization and its work on out-of-school childcare. I also realized that this aspect of childcare was not of direct relevance to my study since out-of-school childcare was mainly for children of school age already attending school. During the visit to the Daycare Trust, I was allowed access to the organization's in-house library. It held many private documents such as correspondence between the organisation and politicians or other childcare interest groups and were of restricted access to the public. I also had

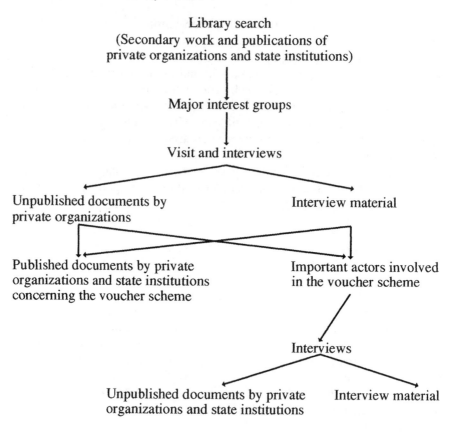

Figure 1.2 The Research Process

informal chats with staff there. The interview in the NCB was conducted with the Information Officer of its Early Childhood Unit. I was surprised to learn that researchers there had been collecting material concerning the voucher scheme. This material included newspaper cuttings, reports of parliamentary debates, publications by government departments and agencies, published or unpublished material by private organizations. They were kept in the in-house library of the Early Childhood Unit. I made many other trips to the organisation to study them. On the whole, although the response rate to my requests for interviews in this first round of communication was not high, the documents and interview material collected were very important and useful. They gave me a more in-depth understanding of the childcare issue. They also provided me with information specific to the voucher scheme. Using this information, I was able to identify those individuals and organizations who had been significantly involved in the voucher issue.

I sent the second round of letters to request interviews in May 1997. Letters were sent to ministers and civil servants from the DfEE, the government department responsible for the voucher scheme; the Labour Party, the major opposition party of the time; local councils and interest organizations. Having learned the lesson from the first round of communication, whenever possible the letters were addressed to the chief executive of an organisation, the chair of a committee, or individual politicians. Their names were identified from various documentary sources as they often had spoken publicly or written about the voucher scheme. The response rate was much better this time. Only the requests made to the then Chief Executive of the NCB, the then Secretary of State for Education and Employment, and civil servants from the DfEE were refused. Six interviews were conducted between June and November 1997. Meetings were held with the then Under-Secretary of State for Education who was responsible for carrying out the voucher scheme; a Labour MP and the then spokesperson for the under-fives; a local councillor and the Chair of the Education Committee of the Local Government Association, who had been the Chair of the Education Committee of the Association of Metropolitan Authorities (AMA), the committee responsible for the voucher issue; and a rebel Conservative local councillor from one of the local councils that considered joining Phase One. Meetings were arranged with the Chief Executive of the PLA as well as the Chief Executive of the NCMA. On both occasions they were changed at short notice due to other business arising at the time of the meeting. As a result I was unable to see the original interviewees but met the Personal Assistant to the Chief Executive of the NCMA and the Publication and Research Manager of the PLA instead.

The interviews were important in clarifying the positions of different actors to the voucher scheme. They helped to make apparent the major points of conflict between actors in the policy process. They also enabled me to experience the physical environment where the debates and the work actually took place. This helped my imagination, and thus my understanding of the issues. There were limitations, though, to the interview data. Firstly, actors as occupants of positions tended to speak in connection with the positions they occupied and the political institutions and interest organizations to which they belonged. They were rather careful about what they said. The views they expressed to me usually resembled the views they had presented to the press and had been recorded in printed material. On issues regarding the collective opinion of the institutions or organizations, they often deferred to their published policy documents or press releases. Secondly, actors usually only knew what they themselves had been doing. They had limited knowledge about what was happening elsewhere, even within their own institutions or organizations. Thirdly, the events in which I was interested had taken place one or two years previously. Actors usually could not recall exactly what had happened and when. They often could only provide very general information of events. Therefore, the interview data provided a partial and fragmented view of the policy process. It had to be supplemented by documentary sources in order to obtain a fuller picture. More documentary sources were gathered through the interviews. They were mainly in the form of unpublished documents from political institutions or private organizations which were of limited access to the public. These included minutes of meetings, briefings of meetings, press releases and correspondence between organizations or individual actors on behalf of organizations.

The documentary sources gathered throughout the research were mainly of four types: published documents by state institutions; published documents by private organizations;[18] unpublished documents by state institutions; and unpublished documents by private organizations. Scott (1990) has suggested four useful criteria to assess documentary sources: authenticity, credibility, representativeness and meaning. The documentary sources used in the study fulfilled these four criteria well. With regard to the criterion of meaning, the majority of the documents were clear and easy to understand. Regarding authenticity, the documents were mostly original copies or photocopies of original ones. They all had a reliable authorship. Regarding credibility, most of the accounts should be considered as sincere. Although they presented different points of view, the differences in opinions were of interest for the study. There was a credibility problem with some newspaper articles which tended to dramatize events or the effect of events. In those circumstances I only used the factual material the articles presented. There was no problem of representativeness concerning the published material. I studied almost all of these documents and had a copy of those I considered useful. It was difficult to assess the representativeness of the unpublished documents. I had the chance to go through those kept in in-house libraries of two organizations. For other unpublished material, it was entirely due to the voluntary acts of the people I talked to that I came to know of its existence. Such material without doubt provided very valuable information for the study. Yet with the vast amount of other material I collected, it was supplementary more than necessary.

No one type of data alone would have been a sufficient source upon which to base the discussion. The book is written and arguments established based on an in-depth analysis of both the documentary sources and the interview material. The reliability of the data used was ensured by cross-referencing with different types of data. Interview material is quoted directly in the discussion a few times only. My original intent was not to include direct quotes, due to my own preference and understanding with regard to how to use the material. It is only on supervisory advice that some interview material is used directly. However, by the time the advice was given the work was in final draft form, consequently it was only possible to fit a few quotations into the text. This may remain a less desirable feature of the work, although it should not affect the findings in any way.

Notes

1   Department for Education and Employment (DfEE) (1999), *Statistics of Education: Children's Day Care Facilities at 31 March 1998 England*, DfEE, London.
2   Ibid.
3   Based on data provided by the DfEE.
4   According to documents provided by the Pre-school Learning Alliance (PLA). Also see chapter 3.
5   The PLA estimated that about 1.8 children used each pre-school place. So the percentage of three- and four-year-olds using pre-schools was approximately 52.06 per cent, according to statistics supplied by the NCB.
6   Daycare Trust (1999a), 'Childcare Gaps', *Childcare Now*, May 1999, Daycare Trust, London.
7   See Thair, T. and Risdon, A., 'Women in the Labour Market: Results from the Spring 1998 Labour Force Survey', *Labour Market Trends*, March 1999.
8   The economically active population comprises people in employment and those unemployed, according to *Labour Market Trends*, March 1996.
9   People in employment are those doing paid work either as an employee or self-employed, those having a job but temporarily away from it, those on government supported training programmes and those who are unpaid family workers. Unemployed people are those without a paid job but available to start work in the next two weeks and have been actively seeking a job in the last four weeks, also according to *Labour Market Trends*, March 1996.
10 Office for National Statistics (1998), *Social Focus on Women and Men*.
11 See for example, Hakim, C. (1995), 'Five Feminist Myths about Women's Employment', *British Journal of Sociology*, vol. 46, no. 3.
12 The Four Demands were: equal pay for equal work; equal education and equal opportunities; free contraception and abortion on demand; free 24-hour community-controlled childcare. The first two demands and part of the third demand have been transferred into national policy: Equal Pay Act 1970, Sex Discrimination Act 1975, Abortion Act 1967, Equal Pay (Amendment) Act 1984. See Marchbank (1996), pp. 9, 14.
13 References to 'actions' and 'decisions' apply equally to inaction and nondecision.
14 It should be noted that the set of policy stages may be different for different policy

issues. See chapter 2.

15   Also see Ham and Hill, 1993; Held, 1995a; Hill, 1997; Smith, 1993.
16   Also see Ham and Hill, 1993; Held, 1995a; Hill, 1997; McLennan, 1995; Smith, 1993.
17   Previously the DFE, now merged with the Department of Employment to become the DfEE.
18   This category includes secondary work by academics and newspaper articles. Published material is included in the Bibliography.

2 Policy Process Analysis

Before looking at the policy process of the voucher scheme, this chapter establishes an analytical schema for the study. It specifies the elements that are involved in the analysis of the policy process. This is achieved through examining some important approaches to the study of the political system and process, as well as other relevant theoretical arguments. Specifically, David Easton's 'systems analysis' and other approaches which focus on the 'process' of policy making, models of British politics, Giddens's structuration theory, and the work on state autonomy and policy networks are discussed.

The chapter first defines and differentiates between policy and the policy process. Whereas 'policy' consists of a course of actions and decisions by policy actors, 'policy process' is the dynamic process in which such actions and decisions are produced. Hence, it is argued that a study of the policy process should involve two dimensions — the 'process' and the 'actors'. A discussion of Easton's systems analysis and other approaches which all focus on the 'process' of policy making, reveals that the 'process' is separated into some highly related but distinct stages. Each requires separate and independent analysis. A review of the models of British politics identifies possible policy actors. A discussion of Giddens's structuration theory suggests that actors' actions and decisions are affected by three elements: previous policy; rules which actors draw on when making decisions and taking actions; and the resource relationships between actors. The policy network literature provides useful analytical tools for the understanding of the resource relationships between policy actors. The literature on state autonomy suggests that state actors have the potential for autonomous action, therefore an analysis of the policy process needs to pay specific attention to their roles and influences in the making of policy decisions.

'Policy' and the 'Policy Process'

There have been many attempts to define 'policy'. Easton suggests that 'a policy ... consists of a web of decisions and actions that allocate ... values'

(1953, p. 130, quoted in Ham and Hill, 1993, p. 11). Heclo considers it as 'a course of action or inaction rather than specific decisions or actions' (1972, p. 84, quoted in Ibid.). Jenkins defines it as 'a set of interrelated decisions ... concerning the selection of goals and the means of achieving them within a specified situation ...' (1978, p. 15, quoted in Ibid.). Hogwood and Gunn, on the other hand, describe it as 'comprising a series of patterns of related decisions to which many circumstances and personal, group, and organizational influences have contributed' (1986, p. 23). Ham and Hill further explain policy as consisting of 'a decision network' which 'may be involved in producing action'. Policy is usually not 'expressed in a single decision', but 'defined in terms of a series of decisions'. These decisions 'change over time', as a result of 'incremental adjustments to earlier decisions', or 'major changes of direction', or feedback from implementation (1993, pp. 12-14).

Despite some varying elements among these definitions, a common theme is that policy involves a course of actions or a web of decisions. It is the output of a political process. Wildavsky, however, argues that policy is not only a product but also a process. Policy refers 'to a process of decision making and also to the product of that process' (1979, p. 387, quoted in Ham and Hill, 1993, p. 14). Burch and Wood (1990), on the other hand, suggest separate definitions for 'policy' and the 'policy process'. They define 'policy' as 'the products of government — what it is that government produces'. This involves two sets of indices: public expenditure programmes and types of policy products. The former refers to the amount of government money allocated to policy programmes. The latter includes three main categories of rules, regulations and public pronouncements. They are laid down in a variety of ways ranging from Acts of Parliament to general statements of intent; public goods and services; and transfer payments. 'Policy process', on the other hand, refers to the 'policy making activities of government'. This implies, first, 'an activity taking place over time', and second, 'an activity that changes and transforms an entity in the course of handling it' (1990, p. 13).

In terms of conceptual clarity and analytical convenience, I consider this last definition which gives 'policy' and the 'policy process' separate meanings the most desirable. In more general terms, 'policy' is the product of policy making. It involves a course of actions or a web of decisions by policy actors. 'Policy process' is the dynamic process in which such actions and decisions are produced (through the activities of policy actors). Hence, the study of the policy process should be concerned with two dimensions — the 'process' and the 'actors'. The following explains these two dimensions in more detail.

Systems Analysis and Process Approaches

First, I want to explain the dimension of the 'process'. To illustrate my arguments, I make use of the systems analysis by David Easton (1965) and the approaches which focus on the process of policy making. Easton's 'systems analysis' is a classical approach to the study of the policy process. Easton adopts a machine analogy and considers the political system as a vast and perpetual conversion process. It takes in demands and support as inputs, out of which decisions and actions are 'produced' as outputs. The outputs return to haunt the system while influencing the inputs of demands and support. This conversion process of the political system is embedded in an 'environment' which consists of other systems — the ecological system, the biological system, the personality system, the social system and the international system. The 'environment' is important in shaping demands and support as inputs. It also has a direct influence on the conversion process (Figure 2.1).

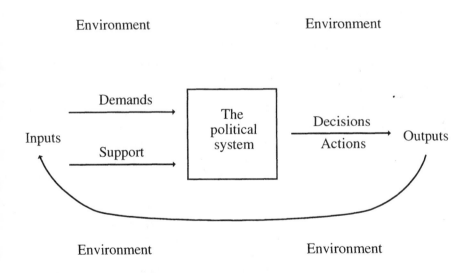

Source: Easton, 1965.

Figure 2.1 A Simplified Model of a Political System

Easton's analysis of the policy process focuses mainly on the input mechanisms of demands and support, the response mechanisms of the political institutions to demands and support, and the feedback mechanisms of the outputs. While highlighting the central importance of the conversion process, relatively little attention is given to its internal mechanisms. In other words, it provides little explanation for how policy decisions are made and how policy actions are produced. Furthermore, the assumption of homogeneity within the conversion process excludes the possibility that there may be difference and conflict within the process, and that the process itself can be a source of input for political action (also see Anderson, 1979; Ham and Hill, 1984, 1993). Nevertheless, the model emphasizes the process of policy making as opposed to institutions or structures. It considers the policy process in three stages: input, output and feedback. Such an approach recognizes the distinctiveness of each of the stages and enables them to be studied independently and attentively.

Analysing the policy process in terms of stages is a rather popular approach taken up by many other scholars of the policy process. Like Easton, they consider the policy process as being separated into some distinct but highly connected stages. They study each of the stages independently and in detail. However, they differ from one another in the ways they define the set of stages. Burch and Wood (1990) suggest that, at the simplest level, there is a distinction between three stages of initiation, formulation and implementation. The initiation stage refers to the generation and early development of a policy proposal. The formulation stage involves the development of a policy in detail. The implementation stage is the carrying out of the policy once it is formally agreed on or approved. Anderson (1975) makes an extension to the simple model and decomposes the policy process into five stages of problem formation, policy formulation, policy adoption, policy implementation and policy evaluation. Hogwood and Gunn (1984) have developed a more complicated set of stages. For them, the policy process involves nine stages: (1) deciding to decide (issue search or agenda setting); (2) deciding how to decide (issue filtration); (3) issue definition; (4) forecasting; (5) setting objectives and priorities; (6) options analysis; (7) policy implementation, monitoring, and control; (8) evaluation and review; (9) policy maintenance, succession, or termination. Burch and Wood (1990), on the other hand, identify policy stages with reference to the activities of officials in dealing with public resources. They recognize three major stages of acquiring resources, dividing resources and applying resources. 'Acquiring resources' refers to the process of extraction and gathering in of public resources from the wider political, economic and social systems. 'Dividing resources' involves the division or allocation of public resources amongst government agencies in terms of policy programmes or policy products. 'Applying resources' is the stage of carrying out policy and receiving impacts, including the distribution of policy benefits and burdens.

To me, the different ways of defining policy stages suggest that, although there are common procedures in policy making, there can be many variations. The policy 'process', the events and discussions involved, and hence the policy stages, can be different for different policy issues. Also, except when constrained by statute requirements, policy events can take place in different sequences on different occasions. Therefore, it is inappropriate to prescribe a set of stages in an analytical model. What is involved should be left open for empirical analysis. Moreover, both the systems model and other process approaches contain the assumption that policy events (hence policy stages) take place in a cyclic order with a uni-directional sequence of cause and effect. This over-simplifies the complexity of the policy process. In the actual world of policy making, different events may happen at the same time, maybe in a different space context. They may influence each other in a multi-directional manner. An empirical analysis requires the methodological awareness that some stages of the policy process need to take account of other stages going on simultaneously.

The policy initiative I am going to study in detail — the Nursery Education Voucher Scheme, exemplifies the above arguments. Six distinct stages can be identified within its policy process. They are, as explained in chapter 1, 'agenda setting', 'option selection', 'legislation', 'policy negotiation', 'implementation' and 'replacement'. Each of these six stages has unique features and distinct implications for the policy initiative. Each of them requires independent and detailed analysis. They are however specific for this policy initiative. The policy process of other policy initiatives may be more conveniently divided into other sets of stages. Also, these six stages did not take place in a uni-directional sequence of cause and effect. After the Government announced its proposal for the voucher scheme, the DfEE carried out negotiation with actors concerned. Following the negotiation stage, the voucher scheme was implemented in pilot areas in Phase One. Meanwhile, legislation was going on simultaneously in Parliament. Issues and discussions which arose during policy negotiation and implementation had an effect on the discussions in Parliament. The result of the legislation process allowed the scheme to go on to Phase Two to be implemented nationwide. Therefore, the three stages of policy negotiation, implementation and legislation influenced each other in a multi-directional manner. The empirical analysis has to take this into consideration.

Finally, it needs to be pointed out that policy stages are seen as real but they do not actually exist. It is only for the purpose of analysis that we consider the policy process as divided into stages.

Models of British Politics and Policy Actors

After explaining the dimension of the 'process', I now discuss the dimension of the 'actors'. I explained earlier that 'policy' is seen as involving a course of actions or a web of decisions by policy actors. Hence, the dimension of the 'actors' contains three questions of concern. First, who are the policy actors? Second, what are their actions and decisions? And third, why do they take such actions and make these decisions? The latter two questions will be considered in later parts of the chapter. In this part of the discussion I concentrate on the first question and look at who the possible policy actors are. 'Policy actors' refer to people who have been involved in the process of policy making and have sought to influence policy decisions. Most of them occupy positions in interest organizations or political institutions. However, in the political process collective decisions are usually made within institutions or organizations to represent collective goals and preferences before negotiating with other organizations or institutions. Therefore, 'policy actors' should also refer to institutions or organizations that are composed of collectives of individual actors. A revision of some models of British politics helps to identify the possible policy actors and their characteristics. These models include the democratic sovereignty model, the party government model, the adversary politics model, the cabinet government model, the bureaucratic dispersion model, the Marxist model and the pluralist model.[1]

The democratic sovereignty model emphasizes the importance of the institutions of representative democracy in policy making — Parliament and local councils. Western democracies have a belief in governance by popular will which is enacted through the institutions of representative democracy with elected representatives at various levels of government. Policy making is characterized by response to and representation of public opinion. This model is especially influential in Britain because of the constitutional importance of Parliament (Greenaway *et al.*, 1992). Parliament's power is constrained only by convention not by constitution. Parliament is the sole law-giving body and Parliamentary sovereignty is indivisible. However, the power of Parliament has been challenged by the power and authority of the Crown, and the need for government to provide good and effective administration. It is further over-shadowed by the political developments in the twentieth century, including 'the rise of well-disciplined parties; the increasing influence of the bureaucracy; the growth of government; the tendency towards delegated legislation; the mushrooming of interest groups;' and the increasing importance of technical expertise (Greenaway *et al.*, 1992, p. 48). The significance of Parliament in the policy process requires careful consideration.

The party government model considers political parties as the key players in the policy process. They control the operations of elected institutions and predominate in the formulation of policy. They mediate public opinion and fuse it into their policy proposals. Government has to act in conformity with the policies and demands of the party in power. These policies are formulated within the party in line with the wishes of party activists and with the party's ideology and values. The party's control of policy making is assured by a manifesto which has been endorsed by the electorate. It is also assured by the concept of a mandate which allows the winner of an election to govern in accordance with its programme and objectives. In Britain, the party government model is reinforced by the existence of a strong two-party system with the Labour Party and the Conservative Party competing for office. At elections the claims of the model tend to be especially significant.

The cabinet government model emphasizes the power and autonomy of the central executive — the Cabinet. It argues that democratic institutions of parties and Parliament are only able to assert influence on policy making on a limited range of issues and never in a sustained manner, usually affecting the timing and the details rather than the substance of policy. In contrast, the Cabinet is at the centre of a vast network of government committees and agencies. It is the central meeting place of bureaucratic conflict and party politics. It is composed of the Prime Minister and other leading members of the government. It is the key co-ordinating force in the policy process. Richardson and Jordan (1987) have pointed out that the Cabinet should not be considered as only consisting of the Prime Minister and the twenty or so ministers. It also includes an elaborate and systematic network of Cabinet Committees, including key standing committees and a number of *ad hoc* committees appointed to deal with particular issues. These are serviced and supported by the ever expanding Cabinet Secretariat.

Whether the extension of its institutional apparatus has strengthened or undermined the Cabinet system is another question of concern. Many have argued that the Cabinet is not unified but segmented or diversified. Ministers stand for policy programmes and fight for financial resources for their own departments. Policy decisions which require interdepartmental co-operation are resolved in Cabinet Committees in which ministers are briefed with policy solutions pre-determined by senior civil servants. The Prime Minister has discretionary power over a wide range of issues including appointing or dismissing Cabinet and Cabinet Committee members, agenda setting, news manipulation, etc. He or she uses this as a means to achieve his or her own policy goals.

Given the segmented nature of the Cabinet, the bureaucratic dispersion model emphasizes the weakness of the centre in co-ordinating policy making. Each of the departments of the state determines policy in its own territory with minimal coordination from the Treasury and the Cabinet Office at the centre. The Cabinet is more a collection of competing departmental heads than a group of mutually supporting and co-operating leaders of the government. Incoherence among departments comes from competition for resources, territory, or protection of departmental interests. This would be most likely to happen when dealing with policies which involve the interests of a number of departments.

When departmental interest is brought into focus, the influential role performed by civil servants cannot be neglected. This is the emphasis of the bureaucratic power model in which paid officials, particularly top civil servants, are seen as major policy makers. Jordan and Richardson (1987) have argued that civil servants are likely to be much more expert than ministers in dealing with departmental affairs. Ministers on average spend only twenty months in any one post. They are also too busy to be involved in all but a tiny proportion of a department's business. Burch and Wood (1990) have also pointed out that civil servants' 'sheer weight of numbers, superior knowledge, control of information, continuity ... and the ability to work away from the glare of publicity' grant them supremacy (p. 38). They are more able to formulate policy according to the reality of governance.

The preceding discussion of the models of British politics revealed the major political institutions in the British political system and their main characteristics. These institutions include Parliament, local councils, the Cabinet (the government Executive), government departments and the Civil Service. The persons involved in these political institutions are MPs, local councillors, the Prime Minister, Cabinet ministers and civil servants. These persons and political institutions are responsible for rule-making and rule-operation. In the words of Weber, they have a 'monopoly of legitimate violence' within a given territory. They constitute the British political 'state' and can also be thought of as 'state actors'.

What has not been stated very clearly in the above models is the role of local councils. Local councils are considered by the democratic sovereignty model as institutions of representative democracy, alongside Parliament. However, the nature of local councils is very different to Parliament. Wilson (1995) summarizes two main roles for local councils. Firstly, they are the 'instruments of democratic self-government', as they are 'the only governmental units beyond the centre that are directly elected by the local population and directly accountable (via elections) to the local electorate'. Secondly, they are 'providers (both directly and indirectly) of a wide range of community services' (p. 230). The attempt of successive Conservative Governments to privatize social services developed the 'enabling role' for local councils: 'local authorities are becoming increasingly important as organizers and contractors and less important as direct service-providers' (p. 232). However, local councils have remained as important providers of services to the local community. They have responsibility for a wide range of local social and economic affairs. National policy made at the centre requires their co-operation in order to be successfully carried out. Therefore, although local councils are political institutions within the state system, their nature is very different from other political institutions. Their rule-making and rule-operation function is restricted to their own local areas. They are located at the periphery of the state not the centre. Their significance in national policy making requires careful examination.

Apart from political institutions, other important actors in the policy process are interest organizations. The significance of interest organizations in policy making is a common theme of the Marxist model and the pluralist model, although they differ in the degree of influence attributed to different groups. In the Marxist model, the political process is dominated by the capitalists and business groups. In the pluralist model, power is distributed among a large number of interest groups and no one group is dominant. In view of these differences, how significant interest organizations are in the policy process is a question for empirical study.

Interest organizations can be divided into 'insiders' and 'outsiders', in terms of their relationships with the government (departments). Insiders are recognized and legitimized by relevant government departments and are consulted on a regular basis. Outsiders, on the contrary, are not accepted by government departments. They do not have a direct involvement in the policy process and can only make their voices heard from a distance (see Jordan and Richardson, 1987; Bagott, 1995). The status of insiders and outsiders may alter with a change of party in government, since some groups are closer to one of the two major political parties than to the other. For example, the trade unions are closer to the Labour Party whereas the right-wing think-tanks are closer to the Conservative Party. So when the Conservative Party is in power, the right-wing think-tanks are insiders but the trade unions are not. Although insiders have the opportunity to be involved directly in policy debates and have the capacity to draw the government's attention to their views, their actual influence on policy decisions is a matter for cautious analysis.

Interest organizations are situated in the civil society outside the state system. These organizations and the persons involved can also be thought of as 'society actors'. The distinction between the state and society, however, is not as clear cut as it might seem. Some actors, like political parties, cut across the state and society. The party government model considers political parties as key players in the policy process. However, political parties should not be regarded as political institutions themselves. This is because they are mainly composed of local and grassroots activists who do not have rule-making and rule-operation functions in a given territory. It is only through success in elections that some party members enter into political institutions and acquire legitimacy in rule-making and rule-operation, locally as local councillors and nationally as MPs. A political party will become most influential in the policy process when it wins a majority of seats in the House of Commons in a General Election and forms a Government. Yet within the party, many grassroots members are distant from the leadership of their parliamentary party and find themselves insignificant in influencing policy making.

There is no consensus as to the relative significance of different actors in the policy process among the models of British politics mentioned above. However, one should not assume any one dominant power in an analytical model. Which actor is relatively more influential and powerful in policy making is an issue for empirical investigation. The elements that are involved in the analysis of the power relationships between policy actors will be discussed in a later part of the chapter.

Structuration Theory and the Production of Action

After looking at the possible policy actors, I shall next explain the other two questions of concern in the dimension of 'actors'. To recap that these two questions are, firstly, what are the actions and decisions of policy actors? And secondly, why do they take such actions and make these decisions? No further explanation is needed for the first of these two questions. What the actions and decisions of policy actors are is simply a question for empirical investigation. Further clarification is necessary to understand why actors undertake certain actions and decisions. Informed by Giddens's theory of structuration,[2] I consider that there can be three aspects to that understanding. Firstly, actors' actions and decisions are affected by previous actions and decisions. Secondly, actors draw upon 'rules' for their actions and decisions. Thirdly, actors' actions and decisions are influenced by their resource relationships with each other. To explain my arguments I shall start by introducing Giddens's conception of action,[3] as illustrated in what he calls the 'stratification model of the acting self (the agent)' (Figure 2.2).

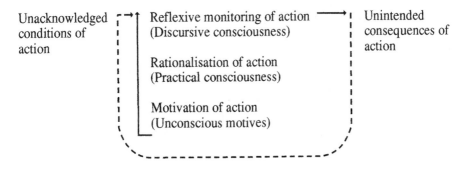

Source: Giddens, 1984.

Figure 2.2 The Stratification Model of the Acting Self

Giddens sees action as a continuous flow. It involves three embedded sets of processes: the motivation of action, the rationalization of action and the reflexive monitoring of action. Action is first prompted by actors' wants — their unconscious motives. Wants have to be consciously taken into consideration and acted on before they can impinge on action. Much of the action occurs through a routine rationalization of what to do. This is based on actors' knowledge of what is going on and how to conduct social activities. Such 'rationalization of action' does not take place in a fully conscious way — usually at the level of 'practical consciousness'. The rationalization of action has to be distinguished from the reflexive monitoring of action. The latter happens when actors discursively systematize and formalize their knowledge, reflect upon their action, monitor it and ground reasons for it. This takes place in a fully conscious way — at the level of 'discursive consciousness'.

Although action is usually intentional (with the rationalization and reflexive monitoring of action), it has unintended consequences. Unintended consequences 'may systematically feed back to be the unacknowledged conditions of further acts' (Giddens, 1984, p. 8; see figure 2.2). In other words, an action has a continual impact on future action. Policy, which consists of actions and decisions by policy actors, continually influences later policy actions and decisions. For example, in the case of the voucher scheme, previous policy had considered care and education for the under-fives as two separate issues. This was one of the factors that contributed to the new policy initiative only being aimed at the expansion of pre-school education. Also, the fact that the reluctance to develop the public sector had encouraged the continual development of the private and voluntary sectors was a reason for allowing publicly-funded vouchers to be used in these sectors. These two examples support the argument that one of the aspects to understanding why policy actors make certain actions and decisions, is to understand the ways in which they are affected by previous policy and its consequences.

Giddens has emphasized that it is a characteristic of human agents that they contain the 'knowledgeability' of how to conduct social activities. All human beings are highly 'learned' in respect of this knowledge. The very core of the knowledge actors incorporate in social encounter is the awareness of the rules of social life. Social rules have the nature of mathematical formulae. While mathematical formulae 'programme' a particular sequence of numbers, social rules 'programme' particular sets or patterns of social activities. An example is the rules of grammar. They are 'formulae for reproducing particular patterns of speech' (Scott, 1995, pp. 208-9). The awareness of social rules is expressed first and foremost in practical consciousness. Actors employ social rules for their action, but they may be unaware, or only partially aware, of these rules. Just as people are usually unaware of the grammatical rules they employ when they speak. Only when actors consciously account for the reasons of their action do they attempt to discursively formulate the 'rules' they draw on.

Giddens's conception of 'rules' is different from the overtly formulated rules from which the term is generally known. Overtly formulated rules are usually written. Examples are, the rules of playing chess, the rules of a selection process, the rules of driving on the road, etc. However, actors do not draw upon overtly formulated rules in their action. They draw upon their *interpretations* of them when they act. Actors' interpretations of overtly formulated rules are social rules in Giddens's sense, but not the formulated rules themselves.

Rules as defined above are referred to as 'structures' by Giddens. Actors draw upon rules for their action; through actors' action the rules are produced and reproduced. They become structural properties embedded in social systems,[4] and mediate the production, reproduction or transformation of the latter. Rules as structures thus exhibit a duality — the rules actors draw upon for their action are at the same time the means of system reproduction.

Understanding the rules actors draw upon is the second aspect to understanding why actors make certain actions and decisions. However, the concept of rules in Giddens's account is too abstract to be useful in empirical study. Further specification of the concept is needed for the analysis of the policy process. What might be the rules actors draw upon in the process of policy making? I consider they could be the values, beliefs, ideologies and interests of policy actors. Values, beliefs, ideologies and interests 'programme' particular sets or patterns of actions and decisions. Actors are usually unaware or only partially aware of the values, beliefs, ideologies or interests they draw upon when they act or decide. Only when actors consciously account for the reasons of their actions and decisions do they become aware of the values, beliefs, ideologies or interests they incorporate. These values, beliefs, ideologies and interests of actors also mediate the production, reproduction or transformation of social systems.

One example of rules is the ideological belief that mothers should stay at home to bolster the family and look after young children. Policy actors' actions and decisions (hence policy) which draw upon this belief would effectively discourage public childcare provision. As a consequence, mothers have to stay at home to look after children. The institution of the traditional family and the gendered division of labour is produced and reproduced through the policy.

Another example of rules is the ideological belief of the New Right that markets should be created for the provision of social services which would otherwise be provided by the public sector. Policy making which draws upon this belief would discourage public provision and encourage the development of the private sector. The system of public social services would be transformed as a consequence.

Actors' inherent interests are also important rules that influence their actions and decisions in policy making. For example, professional organizations usually campaign for policy options which favour the interests of their members, or an MP may oppose a piece of legislation because it is against the interests of his or her constituency. In both situations, the policy actors' actions and decisions may lead to the reproduction or transformation of social institutions or collectives. Their actions and decisions may result in the protection or enhancement (hence reproduction) of their interests, if they have sufficient resources.

The resource relationships between actors is the third aspect to understanding why actors make certain actions and decisions. Giddens thinks that in addition to rules, actors also draw upon 'resources' for their action. Like rules, the awareness of resources is included in the knowledge of the agent. Resources are structures which exhibit duality — actors draw upon their knowledge of resources for their action, through their action resources are produced and reproduced; resources become structural properties embedded in social systems and are the means of system reproduction. Resources also have a quality of their own, as they 'are media through which power is exercised' (Giddens, 1984, p. 16). The control of, or access to, resources allows the actor to make a difference to a specific process or state of affairs, or 'to be able to "act otherwise"' (Ibid., p. 14). In other words, the actor is able to intervene in the action of other actors, or to resist others' intervention.

Giddens does not make the connection between rules and resources very clear. He seems to imply that there is a resource aspect of rules (Scott, 1995). Often when actors act on their interests, they seek to protect or promote their resources. On the other hand, Giddens also suggests that we cannot conceive rules without resources. This is because resources allow the transformative capacity of social rules (see Craib, 1989). For the sake of clarity in analysis, however, it is useful to consider rules and resources as two different aspects which influence action. Rules (including their resource aspect) 'programme' actors' action, but this action may not be able to influence the state of affairs. Whether actors are able to intervene in others' action or resist others' intervention depends on their access to or control over resources, and hence their capacity to exercise power. Therefore, while actors' rules explain why they make certain actions and decisions, actors' control of resources, hence their capacity to exercise power, explains why certain actions and decisions have influence on the state of affairs but some others do not. In this sense rules and resources are also highly connected because actors need sufficient resources for the effect of their rules to be felt. This third aspect of resources and power, as well as the rules of the most powerful, is the most important in understanding why policy is made in certain ways but not in others.

What is missing in Giddens's conceptualization is the explanation of why the access to or control over resources should provide the actor with the capacity to exercise power. It is necessary to consult other relevant literature for further specification of this third aspect of resource relations and power. This is the subject of the next part of the discussion.

Resource Dependency and Power

The literature on policy networks suggests that it is due to the relationships of resource dependency that resources provide actors with the capacity to exercise power. Actors are connected to each other by resource dependency in a policy sector (Benson, 1982) or a policy network (Rhodes, 1986, 1988). Within the sector or network, policy actors have differential access to resources. They do not have access to or control over all the resources they need to survive or function. This is partly due to the division of labour in the policy sector or network (Benson, 1982), and partly due to the stratification of positions actors occupy (Knoke, 1990). Thus, policy actors are reliant upon each other for resources. Those actors who have the crucial resources other actors need, may make use of the resources to exercise power over other actors in order to influence the state of affairs.

Before explaining the above further, it should be noted that the necessary resources in policy making are not only monetary. Rhodes (1988, pp. 90-91) has usefully identified five types of resources that are central to the exchanges that take place in policy sectors or networks. They are authority, money, legitimacy, information and organisation. *Authority* refers to 'the mandatory and discretionary rights to carry out functions or services commonly vested in and between public sector organizations by statute or other constitutional means' (Rhodes, 1988, p. 90). For example, the Prime Minister has the authority to appoint Cabinet members and to oversee the work of the government. Ministers from the Treasury have the authority to control the use of public financial resources. *Money* refers to the funds raised by a public sector organisation from taxes, service charges or fees, borrowing, or some combination of these. They are usually known as public financial resources. *Legitimacy* refers to 'access to public decision-making structures and the right to build public support conferred either by the legitimacy deriving from election or by other accepted means' (Ibid.). For instance, MPs have the legitimacy to make laws and policies that govern society. *Information* refers to 'the possession of data and to control over either its collection or dissemination or both' (Ibid., p. 91). For example, government departments which are responsible for setting out the detail of a policy proposal have control over the information concerning the policy proposal. *Organisation* refers to the possession of people, skills, land, facility and equipment, and hence the ability to act directly without intermediaries. An example is the control that the government has over the vast administrative apparatus of the Civil Service, which provides the organisational resources necessary for consultation and implementation of policy.

The differential access to resources by policy actors is due in part to the division of labour within a policy sector or network (Benson, 1982). Some actors are specialized in providing certain types of resources while other actors are specialized in providing other types. For instance, the Government (through the Treasury) is responsible for the control of public financial resources which are necessary for the expansion of under-fives provision. Pre-schools have the organisational resources to provide education for the under-fives. The Government is dependent on the organisational resources of pre-schools for the expansion of educational provision for the under-fives, whereas pre-schools are dependent on the financial resources controlled by the Government for the expansion of their services. In this way, the Government and the pre-schools are connected to each other by resource dependency.

The differential access to resources is also due to the different positions actors occupy in the policy sector or network. Some positions are more prominent than others and may enjoy centrality and prestige prominence. (Knoke, 1990). *Centrality prominence* explains the quantity of connections. The most central positions in a policy network enjoy many reciprocated ties to other actors (assuming all ties are symmetrical). *Prestige prominence* explains the quality of connections. The most prestigious positions receive many relations but do not, or only very selectively, reciprocate. Those actors who occupy the most prominent positions have the access to the most crucial resources. They are the most depended upon by others for resources. However, when they are out of the positions, they also lose the access to the resources. For instance, the position of a Prime Minister is very prominent and enjoys both centrality and prestige prominence. A Prime Minister has access to some crucial resources in policy making and is heavily depended upon by other actors for resources. When John Major was the Prime Minister, he had access to those resources; but when he lost his office, he also lost the access.

Power is exercised through the differential access to resources and hence resource dependency. Those actors who have access to the most crucial resources upon which other actors have to depend to survive or function may use the resources to exercise power over the latter in order to control the state of affairs. They may intervene in other actors' actions and decisions, or resist others' intervention. Knoke has identified two different ways of using resources to exercise power. In the first instance, 'one actor intentionally transmits information to another that alters the latter's actions from what would have occurred without that information' (Knoke, 1990, p. 3). In the second instance, 'one actor controls the behaviour of another actor by offering or withholding some benefit or harm' (Ibid.). These two instances are not mutually exclusive in a power relationship. On many occasions they exist in a combined manner.

I argued previously that actors need sufficient resources for the effect of their rules to be felt. Thus, the use of resources to exercise power also works to sustain the values, beliefs, ideologies and interests (i.e. rules) of the most powerful actors. As Bachrach and Baratz (1970, p. 7) put it,

> power is exercised when A participates in the making of decisions that affect B. Power is also exercised when A devotes his energies to creating or reinforcing social and political values and institutional practices that limit the scope of the political process to public consideration of only those issues

which are comparatively innocuous to A.

So for Bachrach and Baratz, power has two faces. The first face occurs in observable overt conflicts between actors over decision making. The second face evolves from observable covert conflicts between actors over issues and potential issues. This second face of power works to keep certain issues out of consideration in the policy process. These are issues which would challenge the values, beliefs, ideologies and interests of the most powerful. A decision which involves the second face of power is termed by Bachrach and Baratz as a 'nondecision' (Ibid., p. 44). As will be shown in a later chapter, the concepts of the second face of power and nondecision are useful for understanding why pre-school education, instead of a provision that involved the element of care, became the focus of policy action. It was because the latter contradicted the rules of the most powerful.

This part of the discussion explained the third aspect in the understanding of why actors make certain actions and decisions — resource dependency and power relationship between actors. One form of power relationship in the policy process which has been drawn to the attention of scholars in recent years is the autonomy of state actors in policy making. This is the focus of the next part of the discussion.

State Autonomy and Policy Networks

I indicated in chapter 1 that the theoretical stance of state autonomy is more relevant to the reality of childcare policy making than the other traditions of pluralism or Marxism. In this part of the discussion, I wish to explore further the notion of 'state autonomy' and the explanatory concepts useful for its understanding. I will also briefly look at the ways in which different structures of resource dependency may affect the autonomy of state actors in policy making.

In her article 'Bringing the state back in', Theda Skocpol (in Evans *et al.*, 1985, p. 9) refers to 'state autonomy' as states having the capacity to pursue their own policy goals despite the actual and potential opposition of societal groups:

> States conceived as organizations claiming control over territories and people may formulate and pursue goals that are not simply reflective of the demands or interests of social groups, classes, or society. This is what is usually meant by "state autonomy".

Skocpol explains that states seek to pursue their own goals because of certain identifiable features. These features include the 'extranational orientations' of states — their linkages into transnational structures and into the international community; the challenges states may face in maintaining domestic order; and the organisational resources that collectivities of state officials may be able to deploy (Ibid.). However, state autonomy is not a fixed structural feature of any governmental system. It may come and go and change over time. Whether states are able to act autonomously depends on their 'capacities'. The basic elements underpinning state capacities are 'sheer sovereign integrity', 'stable administrative-military control of a given territory', 'loyal and skilled officials', and 'plentiful financial resources' (Ibid., p. 16). The capacities of states may be uneven across policy areas, and hence unevenly distributed across different government departments or state institutions dealing with different policy areas. Therefore, the extent and the operation of state autonomy requires careful analysis.

Another important work on 'state autonomy' is *On the Autonomy of the Democratic State* by Eric A. Nordlinger (1981). For Nordlinger, the state is autonomous to the extent that it translates its preferences (state preferences) into public policy. He distinguishes different types of state autonomy according to different conditions under which it takes place — when state preferences match societal preferences or when they do not. Here, 'state preferences' is an analytical concept referring to the 'resource-weighted' resultant of public officials' preferences — preferences supported by the variously distributed resources of the state. 'Societal preferences' refers to the resource-weighted resultant of private individuals' preferences. 'Type I state autonomy' occurs when state preferences diverge from societal preferences and state officials act on their own preferences. 'Type II state autonomy' takes place when state preferences diverge from societal preferences and state officials bring about a shift in societal preferences. 'Type III state autonomy' occurs when state preferences and societal preferences are non-divergent and state officials in effect act on their own preferences. There is no state autonomy when state preferences and societal preferences are divergent and state officials are unable to act according to their preferences.

Despite their apparent differences, the definition of state autonomy by Skocpol and that by Nordlinger are complementary to each other. Synthesizing the two, 'state autonomy' denotes the situation where states make policy according to their own preferences and in order to achieve their own goals. However, this notion of state autonomy is unsatisfactory because it involves a conceptual and methodological division between the state and society. (This dichotomy is particularly obvious in Nordlinger's conceptualization.) Such a division gives rise to substantial problems.

First and foremost, as stated in chapter 1, the state is not a unified entity. It is nothing but a set of political institutions involved in rule-making and rule-operation in a given territory. As shown by the models of British politics discussed previously, different political institutions have different characteristics and different functional roles in the political system. State actors occupying different positions in different institutions may work together for a common goal, but they may also have distinctive or even conflicting goals and formulate different policy preferences. In a similar sense, society is not a unified entity either. Society actors are highly diversified. They have different and possibly conflicting goals and different policy preferences. Therefore, the notion of state autonomy is better regarded as shorthand for denoting the situation where a certain group of state actors make policy according to their own policy preferences in order to achieve their own goals, disregarding the preferences and goals of other state actors and society actors. When discussing state autonomy it is important to identify which state actors have the autonomy, and in relation to whom.

Nordlinger's typologies of state autonomy, distinguishing the different circumstances in which state autonomy occurs, are potentially helpful for our understanding. However, the state-society dichotomy embedded in his conceptualization needs to be removed in order for the typologies to be useful. The modified typologies are as following. Type I* state autonomy occurs when the policy preferences of a certain group of state actors diverge from the preferences of other state actors or actors in society, and the group of state actors act on their own preferences. Type II* state autonomy occurs when the policy preferences of a certain group of state actors diverge from the preferences of other state actors or actors in society, and the group of state actors bring about a shift in the preferences of other state actors or actors in society. Type III* state autonomy occurs when the policy preferences of a certain group of state actors are non-divergent from the preferences of other state actors or actors in society, and the group of state actors in effect act on their own preferences. There is no state autonomy when the policy preferences of the group of state actors concerned are divergent from the preferences of other state actors or actors in society, and the group are unable to act according to their own preferences.

Nordlinger's typologies (and hence their modifications) do not provide the explanation as to why the state actors can or cannot act autonomously in those circumstances described. Such an explanation can be made by using concepts of resource dependency and power introduced in the last part of the discussion. When type I* state autonomy occurs, certain state actors are able to resist the intervention of other state actors and society actors in policy making. When type II* state autonomy occurs, certain state actors are able to intervene in or make a change to other state actors' and society actors' policy preferences. In both situations, the group of state actors who are autonomous have access to the crucial resources upon which other state actors and society actors have to depend in order to survive or function. The group of state actors manipulate those resources to exercise power over other actors in order to act on their own policy preferences and pursue their own goals. When type III* state autonomy occurs, the policy preferences of the group of more resourceful state actors are more or less the same as those of other state actors and society actors. The group in effect act on their own preferences.

In the situation where there is no state autonomy, the group of state actors concerned are unable to act according to their policy preferences. Their autonomy is challenged because they have to depend on the resources of other state actors and society actors for the success of their policy. In order to achieve their goals, the group of state actors may modify their policy preferences to bring them more into line with the preferences of other state actors or society actors in exchange for the resources they need. The extent to which they diversify their preferences affects the extent of resource exchange.

The structure of resource dependency, hence the type of the policy network involved in the policy process, may affect the autonomy of the state actors. Following Benson (1982) and Rhodes (1986), a policy network is a complex of policy actors connected to each other by resource dependency. It is distinguished from other networks by breaks in the structures of resource dependency. Thus, different types of networks may be identified according to different structures of resource dependency. For Rhodes (1988), the structures of resource dependency, hence the types of networks, vary along five dimensions of constellation of interest, membership, vertical interdependence, horizontal interdependence and distribution of resources. Whereas vertical interdependence refers to the intra-network relationships, horizontal interdependence is about the relationships between policy networks.

The different types of networks can be seen as being located along a continuum with policy communities and issue networks at either end (Marsh and Rhodes, 1992). Policy communities and issue networks are two ideal types of policy network with two extreme and contradictory structures of resource dependency. Policy communities are characterised by the continuity of a highly restrictive membership, sharing of interests, high degree of vertical interdependence based on shared service delivery responsibilities, and limited horizontal articulation with insulation from other networks. Issue networks are characterised by a large number of participants, unstable membership, varied interests, unequal distribution of resources and a limited degree of interdependence.

Using the two ideal types of networks as examples, Smith (1993) has argued that the type of network may affect the level of state autonomy (Table 2.1). Policy communities may increase the autonomy of state actors by creating infrastructural power — the capacity of state actors to penetrate civil society. The high degree of interdependence of state actors and society actors establishes the means through which state actors can intervene in society. The limited degree of horizontal articulation isolates the policy community and excludes other state actors and society actors outside the community from participating in the policy process. This enhances the autonomy of both the state actors and society actors within the community. However, policy communities can decrease the autonomy of state actors. This occurs when the high degree of interdependence leads to the 'capture' of state actors by interest groups. Interest groups dominate the policy community and the policy making process.

Table 2.1 Policy Networks and State Autonomy

Level of autonomy	Policy network	
	Policy community	Issue network
High	High degree of interdependence producing infrastructural power.	Many actors in conflict, high level of freedom.
Low	High degree of interdependence, interest group capture.	Many actors, limited control.

Source: Smith, 1993.

Issue networks may increase state autonomy when the conflict between groups provides state actors with high level of freedom to act on their own policy preferences. In contrast, issue networks may decrease state autonomy if the presence of many loosely connected actors makes the control of state actors over the policy process difficult. In this latter case, issue networks reduce the infrastructural power of state actors and limit their control over policy making.

The four situations discussed above are based on the two ideal types of networks. In the actual situation, as the structures of resource dependency vary, the ways in which they would affect the autonomy of the state actors should also vary. Therefore, the four situations should be seen as guidelines for empirical analysis, but not fixed structural features of networks.

Towards an Analytical Schema

In this chapter, I discussed the various elements of concern for the analysis of the policy process. While 'policy' is the actions and decisions of policy actors, the 'policy process' is the dynamic process in which actions are produced and decisions are made. Hence, there are two dimensions in the analysis of the policy process — the process and the actors (Figure 1.1). The 'process' refers to the dynamic process of policy making. It is separated into some distinct but highly related stages. Each of these stages has a unique function in the policy process and distinct implications for policy outcomes. Each of them requires separate and independent analysis. Policy stages may not take place in a cyclical order of cause and effect. Certain stages may take place simultaneously with some others. The process, the events and discussions involved are different for different policy issues. Therefore, the set of policy stages should be specific and is an issue for empirical analysis.

The dimension of 'actors' is concerned with the participation of policy actors in the policy process and their attempts to influence policy decision making. The term 'policy actors' refers to persons occupying positions in political institutions and interest organizations, as well as these institutions and organizations themselves. The analysis along the actors' dimension is concerned with three questions. Firstly, who are the policy actors? Secondly, what are their actions and decisions? Thirdly, why do they take such actions and make these decisions? There are three further aspects to the understanding of the last question. They are, the influence of previous policy and its consequences; the 'rules', i.e. values, beliefs, ideologies and interests, that actors draw upon for their actions and decisions; and the relationships of resource dependency and power between actors.

The analysis of the policy process needs to pay specific attention to the roles and influences of state actors in policy making. This is because state actors have the potential for autonomous action. They have the capacity to make policy decisions according to their own policy preferences and goals. However, the state is not a unified entity. The analysis of state autonomy needs to clarify which state actors have the autonomy, and in relation to whom. The analysis should also pay attention to the ways in which the structure of resource dependency, hence the type of policy network, affects the autonomy of the state actors.

Notes

1   For a more detailed discussion of these models, see Greenaway, *et al.*, 1992; and Burch and Wood, 1990.

2   For a summary of the theory see Giddens (1984), *The Constitution of Society*, chapter 1.

3   Although Giddens's theory is about the production of action, it should also be relevant for the making of decisions. While the production of action involves the making of decisions, making a decision itself is an action.

4   In Giddens's sense, social systems are composed of sets of interdependent institutions and collectivities. Institutions are those social practices that are most deeply embedded in time and space, such as the institution of marriage.

3 The Policy and Provision of Childcare

I have argued in both chapter one and two that one of the aspects to understanding why policy actors make certain actions and decisions (hence policy) is the influence of previous policy and its consequences. In this chapter, I would like to review the history of childcare policy and childcare provision, from the earliest days to the present time. The purpose is to identify the issues that were to influence the voucher scheme, and to demonstrate the continuity of these issues.

The history of childcare will be considered in five parts: 'Earliest Childcare', 'Post-War Developments', 'The Thatcher Era', 'The Major Period' and 'Policy under New Labour'. 'Earliest Childcare' is concerned with the earliest development of institutionalized childcare provision at the beginning of the twentieth century, and the development of childcare policy and provision during the two World Wars. 'Post-War Developments' describes government policy and the development of childcare provision from the end of the Second World War to the time when Mrs. Thatcher became the Prime Minister. 'The Thatcher Era' looks at the policy of the successive Thatcher Governments and the development of provision during that time. 'The Major Period' covers the policy and provision of childcare in the period when John Major was the Prime Minister. Finally, 'Policy under New Labour' looks at the policy of the Government at the time of writing — Tony Blair's (New) Labour Government, on childcare provision.

Earliest Childcare

In the pre-industrial era childcare was shared within the extended family. With industrialization the nuclear family was gradually loosened from its kinship network, and the family was gradually separated from the 'productive' sphere of work. Childcare was thus separated from its traditional familial setting and the mother became the main carer in the nuclear family. For working mothers, the first institutionalized childcare facilities were developed in the early nineteenth century.[1] One form of these was the 'dame school', the predecessor of day nursery. Dame schools were private and profit-making, packing in as many children as possible. In common with day nurseries they only provided daycare. Other forms were oriented to the educational benefit of young children. Some were opened by enlightened employers for the children of their employees. There were kindergartens based on the methods of child development by the German educator Fröbel. These were few in number, mostly private and attended by middle-class children. There were also 'infant schools' which were the earliest form of public provision of pre-school education. They were voluntarily attended by children over the age of three from various backgrounds. Educational provision experienced a rapid expansion towards the end of the nineteenth century. When all public elementary schooling became free of charge in 1891, there was a marked increase in the number of infant schools within elementary schools. Around the turn of the century almost half of the three- and four-year-olds were attending some kind of pre-school education. However, the number of infant schools dropped drastically from the beginning of the new century. This was due to the decrease in the number of women workers, and the increased burden on local governments after compulsory education for all children over five was enacted in 1870.

The first involvement of the public sector in day nursery provision was triggered by the First World War in 1914-1918. The need for women to work for the war effort brought an expansion of childcare provision in all sectors, most importantly, in the public sector. Over 100 day nurseries were set up across the country. They only provided care for children when their mothers were working in the factories. Most of these facilities were disbanded after the war. The few which remained were brought under the jurisdiction of welfare departments of local authorities in accordance with the Maternity and Child Welfare Act 1918. The Act empowered local authorities to establish or to maintain day nurseries. A separate Education Act of the same year gave LEAs the power to establish and maintain nursery schools and classes. Neither legislation led to significant development in either type of provision. By 1938, there were about 4,000 places in public day nurseries and just over 9,500 in nursery schools or classes (Cohen and Fraser, 1991). Although a distinction between facilities which were aimed at educating young children and those which mainly provided care did exist at that time, these two pieces of legislation established the foundation for the functional and institutional separation of care and education for the under-fives (Ruggie, 1984). As we will see later in the discussion, this separation continued throughout the rest of the century. It had significant implications for the further development of childcare policy and provision.

It was not until the Second World War that the next extensive expansion in public childcare provision took place. As was the case in the First World War, women were drafted into factories to aid the war effort. Over 1600 local authority day nurseries were set up to assist women workers with childcare (Ginsburg, 1992). By the end of the war, there were 62,000 nursery places for children in England and Wales, more than double the number of places available in 1988. There were similar developments in Scotland and Northern Ireland (Cohen and Fraser, 1991). However, towards the end of the War, local authority day nurseries began to be closed down.

Post-War Developments

After the War, the central government halved its grant for day nurseries to local authorities. Buildings which had been requisitioned for nursery use were returned to their previous uses (Randall, 1995). By the early 1950s, only a few hundred local authority day nurseries remained open (Ginsburg, 1992). The massive closure reflected the view that women should withdraw from the workforce when wartime needs were over. Such a view was reinforced by the post-war child-rearing theory that early separation of mother and child was dangerous and should be avoided (Cohen and Fraser, 1991). Influenced by such an ideology of motherhood, public policy for childcare after the War emphasized the responsibility of mothers to look after young children. Publicly-funded services were only responsible for the care of children who were 'in need', and the education of older three- and four-year-olds. This policy was expressed in the Ministry of Health's circular issued the very month the war ended. It says,

> in the interest of the health and development of the child no less than for the benefit of the mother, the proper place for a child under two is at home with his mother ... the right policy to pursue would be positively to discourage mothers of children under two from going out to work; to make provisions for children between two and five by way of nursery schools and classes; and to regard day nurseries as supplements to meet the special needs of children whose mothers are constrained by individual circumstances to go out to work or whose home circumstances are in themselves unsatisfactory from the health point of view or whose mothers are incapable for some good reason of undertaking the full care of their children. (Ministry of Health, circular 221/45, quoted in Ginsburg, 1992, p. 172).

As we will see later in the discussion, the above sentiments remained as the basic principles of childcare policy in the succeeding fifty years. The ideology of motherhood continued to be an important rule influencing policy, particularly under the Conservative administrations. The intention to provide pre-school education for all children between two and five years-old was mentioned again in the 1970s and the 1990s, but this goal has never been achieved.

In the twenty years or so after the Ministry of Health's circular, public childcare provision was in an almost inert state. By 1963, thirteen County Councils and thirteen County Boroughs had actually closed down all of their nurseries.[2] However, at the same time, the socioeconomic situation had undergone significant changes. The number of women in paid employment had increased steadily from 7 million or 31 per cent of the labour force in 1951, to 9 million to make up 35.6 per cent of the labour force in 1971. This figure included women with young children, who were becoming increasingly involved in paid work. The demand for childcare facilities rose as a consequence, and was too great for the limited public provision. Meanwhile, there were significant developments in the child-centred professions — child psychology, education, social work, etc. They were increasingly concerned with the needs of children, and the crucial importance of a healthy childhood for an individual's subsequent emotional and intellectual development.

With the changed socioeconomic situation, the issue of childcare provision received heightened official attention. This was expressed through three significant government reports. They were the Plowden Report on primary education by the Central Advisory Council for Education (England) in 1967; the Seebohm Report on the organisation of local authority social services in 1968; and the Finer Report on one-parent families in 1974. The Plowden Report suggested public provision of nursery education on demand for the three- and four-year-olds. The provision should be on a part-time basis because a child should not be separated from the mother for a whole day. The Seebohm Report also expressed the concern about the effect of prolonged separation of young children from their mothers. Nevertheless, it suggested some increase in local authority day nursery places. It also recommended the provision of care for nursery school children outside school hours, and a better co-ordination of different types of provision for pre-school children. Lastly, the Finer Report recognized the urgent need for a considerable expansion in public provision or support for daycare services for children under five, in view of the increase in the number of one-parent families.

Following these recommendations, there were a series of new policy initiatives. On the education front, the Government included nursery education projects in the Urban Aid Programme from 1968. Three million pounds were provided to be spent on facilities for children under five in urban areas designated as deprived. An education White Paper was issued by the Department of Education in 1972, under the then Minister of Education, Mrs. Thatcher. It generally accepted the arguments of the Plowden Report and announced the Government's goal to expand nursery education in order to meet the demands of all three- and four-year-olds by 1982. A sum of 17.2 million pounds was made available for a new building programme for nursery schools in the financial year 1974-75. On the care front, following the reorganization of local authority social services, in 1972, the Department of Health and Social Security (DHSS) requested that the new local authority departments submit ten-year development plans for daycare provision. The DHSS set out a target of eight day nursery places for every 1,000 children under five.

Alongside these policy developments was the constant influence of the ideology of motherhood and the subsequent view that the best place for young children was at home with their mothers. Public provision that involved the aspect of care was repeatedly prioritized for children who were 'in need'. This was re-emphasized in the Ministry of Health's circular in 1968. It stated that 'wherever possible the younger pre-school child should be at home with the mother ... because early and prolonged separation from the mother is detrimental to the child'. The priority groups for publicly-funded daycare provision included children of 'lone parents who have no option but to go out to work'; children who needed 'temporary daycare on account of the mother's illness'; 'whose mothers are unable to look after them adequately'; and for whom 'daycare might prevent the breakdown of the mother or the break-up of the family' (Ministry of Health, 1968, quoted in Moss, 1991, p. 133). Essentially the provision was limited to children whose parents (mothers in particular) were unable to provide proper childcare and needed help.

Before any real expansion in public childcare provision could be made based on the policy initiatives developed in the late 1960s and early 1970s, there was a change of government in 1974. Although the incoming Labour Government did not explicitly proclaim the ideology of motherhood, it was unmoved by the pressures upon it for childcare provision. It believed in the need to control public spending and held a firm position in restraining the growth of the welfare state (Ginsburg, 1992). They introduced severe cut backs to public expenditure. The capital programme for local authority social service departments as a whole was cut by 20 per cent in 1974. The central government funding for nursery education building programme for 1975-76 was almost half that of the previous year (see Randall, 1995). Provision for the under-fives became an early victim of the restraint in public expenditure.

Against the hesitant development in the public sector, the private and voluntary sectors experienced significant expansion. The growth was driven by the perpetual increase in the demand for childcare facilities. It received support from successive governments. The number of places with registered childminders in England and Wales increased from 1,700 in 1949 to 47,200 in 1968. Childminding is a type of service provided by individuals who care for other people's children in their own home. Successive governments had supported childminding as an alternative to public daycare services. Childminding regulations were extended in 1968. Registration requirements were tightened and local authorities were empowered to provide more support for childminders (Cohen and Fraser, 1991). The Labour Government in 1976 restated its support for childminding (DHSS, 1976, see Ginsburg, 1992). A circular in 1978 asked local authorities to review their support and advice services, including in-service training, for childminders. It stated that the Government supported the development of childminding because of its low cost and flexibility for working parents to suit hours of work. The Government believed that children under three were too young to benefit from group care as provided by nurseries. On the contrary, childminding was a type of care closest to the 'ideal' of children being cared for by their own mothers. A good childminder could provide care 'that is the nearest substitute to the child's own home' and 'is more in tune with his limited capacity for social contacts than the communal experience of a day nursery' (DHSS/DES, 1978, quoted in Moss, 1991, p. 134). A limited amount of money was made available to support innovative projects for childminding (Cohen and Fraser, 1991). A national body, the NCMA, was established in 1977 by a group of childminders, parents and other interested people to promote and advance childminding.[3]

Voluntary playgroups had also experienced significant growth since the beginning of the playgroup movement in the mid-1960s. Playgroups provide sessional care and education for children aged between three and five. Most of them run for a few half days a week. Playgroups were first started by mothers who recognized the need for their children to play in the company of other children. Without public nursery places, they established playgroups themselves. In 1961 a London mother wrote to *The Guardian* about how she started a playgroup of her own. She received an overwhelming response from people wanting to set up such groups or already running them. She put these people in contact with each other. In August 1962, 150 of them held the first Annual General Meeting (AGM) of the Pre-school Playgroup Association (PPA).[4] Five years later its membership had increased to 2,200 and it received funding from the government for the first time.[5] Government policy towards playgroups had evolved in a favourable manner. Playgroups were seen as providing diversity and choice. With their low public cost, some local authorities had used playgroups as a substitute to publicly-funded nursery education provision (Cohen and Fraser, 1991).

Besides childminding and playgroups, other independent provision, such as private nurseries, experienced growth too. As we will see later in the discussion, this trend continued with the perpetual reluctance of the government to develop the public sector and the sustained increase in the demand for childcare facilities. The continual expansion of the independent sector had significant implications for the development of childcare policy and provision that followed.

The Thatcher Era

The Thatcher Government came to office in 1979. Its approach to public policy popularized the New Right Ideology. Although there are many facets to New Right thinking (see Ashford, 1993), the Ideology has been distilled into two main strands — economic liberalism and social conservatism (Abbott and Wallace, 1992; Jordan, 1993). Economic liberalism advocates limited government and free market forces. This is usually expressed through those policies of lowering inflation, reducing taxation, privatization of public social services, introducing markets to the public sector and deregulation. Social conservatism argues for social order and authority based on traditional social, religious and moral views. It is often expressed in those policies that reinforce traditional family values (including the gendered division of labour and the ideology of motherhood), encourage the division of the public and the private spheres, and advocate public non-intervention in private family matters. It has been suggested that the Thatcher Government's policy may not have been wholly stimulated by the New Right thinking. Mrs. Thatcher was 'best seen as selecting from the New Right menu only these items that suited her preformed world view' (Jordan, 1993, p. 5). Nevertheless, the Thatcher Government's approach to childcare was certainly compatible with the New Right Ideology. This was because it involved a policy to create a market for childcare provision, i.e. to discourage public provision and to encourage independent provision; and to regard daycare as a private family matter.

It can be seen from the previous discussion that the Thatcher Government's approach to childcare was not entirely new. Previous governments had been discouraging public provision and encouraging independent provision. The Thatcher Government's policy in effect enhanced previous policy by suggesting a market solution to the limited public provision, and by explicitly considering daycare as essentially a private family matter. The latter view was only implicitly reflected in earlier policy statements, by saying that the best place for young children was at home with their mothers. It was made explicit in 1985 by a junior minister responsible for child daycare services in the Department of Health (DoH). 'Daycare will continue,' he commented, 'to be primarily a matter for private arrangement between parents and private and voluntary resources, except where there are special needs' (John Patten, *Hansard*, 18 February 1985, Col. 397, quoted in Moss, 1991, p. 133).

Active discouragement of public provision was enacted through a series of policy actions. The goal set out by the 1972 Education White Paper (under Mrs. Thatcher herself who, at that time, was the Minister for Education) for a universal provision for three- and four-year-olds was abandoned. The 1980 Education Act removed the obligation of LEAs to consider nursery education needs (Ginsburg, 1992). The Minister of Education, Sir Keith Joseph, made it clear in 1981 that it was not the duty of the government to secure a national provision for every child under five. Moreover, the Government introduced the Rates Bill in 1984. The purpose of the bill was to bring about massive reductions in local government spending. Selective rate limitation (rate-capping) was applied to those local authorities which exceeded approved levels of expenditure. This was the most extreme example of a range of devices used by the central government to control local expenditure. The most immediate and severe effect of this new policy was on non-statutory services such as childcare provision (also see Mottershead, 1988). A white paper in 1985 further confirmed that the Government did not encourage local governments to use public funding to expand childcare provision. It stated, 'plans for local authority expenditure should allow provision to continue in broad terms within broadly the same total as today' (quoted in Randall, 1996, p. 180).

In addition to restraining public expenditure and discouraging the development of public provision, the Government also introduced measures to increase tax revenue, which in effect attacked parents and discouraged employer provision of childcare. The 1984 Finance Bill introduced income tax on the benefits parents received in the form of subsidized places at a workplace nursery. In some cases it made demands for back-tax for up to six years. A sizeable campaign was mounted against the policy. This led the Treasury to announce in April 1985 that the back-tax would not be collected, but benefits in the future would incur tax. Attempts to amend the Finance Bill in subsequent years were not successful (see Mottershead, 1988). It was not until the 1990 budget that the policy was abolished (Cohen, 1990). I will return to this point later.

Within such an unfavourable policy environment, there were some piecemeal official efforts. The DHSS announced the Under-Fives Initiative in 1982. Central government funding was made available for voluntary bodies working with children and their families. The purpose of the funding was to assist in the development of new schemes. It was again mainly targeted at 'disadvantaged families' — families of single parents, of low income, those having problems coping with young children, or those from ethnic communities. The initiative was allocated two million pounds each year starting from the financial year 1983/84. The funding was initially planned for three years. Projects developed were expected to be taken up by other funding bodies afterwards. A smaller amount of money was later provided for another two years for those projects unable to get other means of support. The original funding was distributed according to a variety of 'typologies' of services — family support, training, public education, etc., only 20.3 per cent was allocated for childcare provision (mainly daycare). With an annual government expenditure of many billions of pounds, two million a year was too small to be traced through the national accounts, not to mention the fraction allocated to childcare. This probably did not represent a net increase in government spending on childcare provision when taken with the substantial cutbacks in central government expenditure on local authorities (Mottershead, 1988).

Another official effort was the Information Scheme. Following a visit to the United States of America by two officers from the DHSS in 1984, ministers were impressed by the Californian system of Resource and Referral Centres to provide information for parents. They expressed their willingness to develop similar pilot schemes in the United Kingdom, to be run by voluntary agencies. The only successfully developed scheme was the Sheffield scheme proposed by the NCMA. It received funding for three years from the DHSS from December 1986. While many local authorities already provided useful guides to childcare in their areas, such a scheme did nothing to help solve the insufficient public provision. As Mottershead commented (1988, p. 28), 'if one of the problems about childcare is that there is not generally enough of it ..., then providing more information about an inadequate level of provision may not be seen as particularly helpful'.

These piecemeal efforts had no real effect on the advancement of public childcare provision, and there was no real acceptance of such a policy. It was not until the end of the 1980s that officials came to appreciate the need to improve both the quantity and quality of childcare provision. This change in attitude could be seen as the result of a number of factors.[6] The policy developments in the first half of the 1970s to expand nursery education and daycare provision, had a long term influence. Other developments such as the increasing number of lone mothers and the rising participation of women in the labour market, had effects too. The proportion of families with dependent children headed by a single mother continued to increase. It was approximately 12.5 per cent by 1987. The number of women in paid employment also grew continually. For women with pre-school children, the rate increased from 24 per cent in 1983 to 35 per cent in 1987, although only 11 per cent of the latter were in full-time employment.[7] Both developments heightened the demand for childcare facilities. There was also an increased recognition of the significance of childcare in aiding women's employment prospects. During the 1980s there were a number of feminist-inspired childcare campaigns (See Lovenduski and Randall, 1993). Feminists and their ideas also influenced the trade unions and Labour-controlled local councils, encouraging the introduction and expansion of childcare programmes within these organizations.

In addition to the social and economic developments which had already taken place, there was concern over the demographic time-bomb. The Department of Employment released figures in May 1988, followed by the report of the National Economic Development Council in December, which predicted that by 1993, the number of school-leavers, i.e. potential participants in the labour market, would fall by nearly a third. Although the number was due to rise again by the mid-1990s, it would not reach the level of the early 1980s. Most new jobs would have to be taken up by women who were currently economically inactive. Furthermore, there was evidence of skill shortage across the country. Recruitment difficulties were significant in some portions of the labour market. Both the Government and employers had to persuade mothers of young children, especially those with badly needed skills, to return to the labour market. Heightened official and employer attention to the issue was reinforced by the move to the completion of the single European market by 1992. With Britain's poor record in childcare provision, it could mean even greater difficulty in recruiting within a European labour market (Cohen, 1990).

Towards the end of the period of Thatcher rule there was a significant increase in state activity in relation to the issue of childcare provision. However, discussion continued to sharply divide the issues of care and education. Little was done to tackle the problem of insufficient financial resources which was essential for the expansion of provision. Consequently, there was no real expansion in public provision.

In January 1989, after conducting an inquiry into educational provision for the under-fives, the House of Commons Select Committee on Education, Science and Arts published its report, *Educational Provision for the Under-Fives*. It called for a commitment by central and local governments to the steady expansion of nursery education for all three- and four-year-olds (HC Paper no. 30-I, session 1988-89). It urged a resumption of the target of universal provision set out by the 1972 education White Paper. It recommended improvements in the training opportunities for people working with the under-fives; the establishment of a recognized framework of qualifications; the inclusion of under-fives specialists in discussions on the new national curriculum; and improvements in the educational content of the care given to under-fives in local authority day nurseries and independent pre-schools/playgroups. It also suggested a joint departmental survey to inquire into the existing demand and provision for the under-fives.

In response to the House of Commons education committee's proposals, the Government set up a committee in the Department of Education and Science (DES) to examine the educational experience of pre-school children. The committee was chaired by the then education minister Angela Rumbold. The Rumbold Report was published in 1990. It made many astute observations and stressed the need for improvements in coordination, but it failed to address the fundamental issue of the lack of financial resources needed to expand provision.

The Government announced a 'five-point programme' for developing childcare provision in March 1989. This was the outcome of the work of the Ministerial Group on Women's Issues. This inter-departmental group had been meeting since 1986 and was initially under the Home Office. The 'five-point programme' was described as 'designed to pave the way for the provision of childcare[8] which meets the needs of the family' (quoted in Cohen, 1990, p. 31). The five points included amendments to the Children's Bill (now the Children Act 1989) to improve the registration and enforcement procedures for day nurseries, childminders and playgroups; guidance to LEAs and school governors to encourage the use of school premises for after school and holiday play schemes; encouragement for a voluntary accreditation scheme to guarantee quality; support for the voluntary sector through pump-priming of projects and encouragement of partnerships with employers; and encouragement for employers to use the tax relief available to provide childcare. Again, there was no mention of the financial resources that were needed for any possible development of provision.

A national research and development project, Working with Under Sevens, was established in May 1989. The purpose of the project was to prepare recommendations for new forms of national vocational qualifications in childcare. Setting up a framework of qualifications was one of the recommendations suggested by the report of the House of Commons education committee. The project was part of a broader Care Sector Consortium set up by the Training Agency. Its work involved examination of the range of occupations of those working with under-sevens and their families, the functions they carried out, the skills they required and the standards they should meet. The project prepared a set of standards which would offer considerable potential for widening access to childcare work, and for improving the status of it. The initiative revealed an increasing official emphasis on the quality of provision for young children. However, there was criticism that the exercise was carried out with too much haste and that too few financial resources were available for its implementation (see Cohen, 1990).

Following the suggestions in the 'five-point programme' made by the Ministerial Group on Women's Issues, the DES issued a circular on the use of school premises in England in October 1989. The circular was issued in slightly different forms elsewhere in the United Kingdom. It encouraged LEAs and School Governing Boards to offer their premises for the use of after school clubs and holiday play schemes. However, the use of school premises was expected to carry a charge. In drawing attention to the need for schools to charge an economic rent, the new arrangement actually jeopardized some existing schemes which had had the use of school premises at a very low rent or at no charge. The KCN reported that there was little response to this circular (see Cohen, 1990).

A second Under-Fives Initiative was launched to run from 1989 to 1992. Two million pounds were allocated to voluntary organizations for the funding of projects. These included a European Commission Childcare Action Project on individual care-givers developed by Working for Children in Wandsworth. The new financial support was concentrated on daycare. With its limited amount of funding, it was targeted particularly at families living in temporary accommodation. In other words, the money available only benefited families that were 'in need'. This was consistent with the official principle that public provision of care was only for children and families who had special needs.

In December 1989, the Office of Population Censuses and Surveys was asked by Parliament to undertake a survey to obtain the picture of parental arrangements for childcare (including the use of educational facilities) for children under eight. The survey gathered information on the pattern of attendance at day nurseries, nursery schools and classes, primary schools and playgroups, and the use of childminders, relatives and friends who looked after the children. Information was also collected on parental preferences, as well as arrangements for school-age children after school hours and during school holidays (*Hansard*, 5 December 1989, Col. 137). As most of the national research had previously concentrated on the provision of childcare services, this survey provided a useful measurement of the use and demand for childcare facilities. However, it had no effect on the expansion of provision with neither follow-up initiatives nor extra financial resources.

As mentioned previously, the Government rescinded the taxation on the benefit of workplace nursery places provided by employers in the 1990 Budget. Such a move could be seen as seeking to encourage employers to provide childcare, as part of a response to the issue of the demographic time-bomb. However, other than placing increasing emphasis on employer provision of childcare, the Government provided little other assistance for employers (see Cohen, 1990).

The most important policy development for the childcare sector under the Thatcher administration was the Children Act 1989. It began with a consultation paper in 1985, the Act itself was announced in 1989 and was implemented in October 1991. The Lord Chancellor described it as the 'most comprehensive and far-reaching reform of child care law which has come before Parliament in living memory' (quoted in Bull *et al.*, 1994, p. 5). The Act sought to unite a fragmented body of public and private law under a single statute in order to provide 'a single, rationalized child care system, with all legal remedies available in all cases' (Fox-Harding, 1991, quoted in Ibid.). Within its broad remit, there was no mention of the education of pre-school children. Sections within Part III 'Local Authority Support for Children and Families', and Part X 'Childminding and Day Care for Young Children' dealt specifically with daycare services for children aged under eight. It gave local authorities three main duties: to regulate provision offered by the private and the voluntary sectors; to coordinate provision made by different agencies; and to provide services for children in need. More specifically, local authorities were required (in Ibid., p. 7)

- to regulate the majority of private and voluntary daycare services (Part X);
- to conduct a review of daycare provision used by under-eights in the area at least once every three years (Section 19);
- to provide daycare (and other) services for children who are in need and their families (Sections 17,18), to publicize the services available to families with children in need, and to have regard for the different racial groups in the area to which children in need belong (Schedule 2).

Local authorities were also empowered to provide daycare for children not in need (Section 18), and to provide support services (facilities such as training, guidance and counselling) for adults working in a daycare setting (Section 18), but there was no requirement that they should do so.

The Children Act was praised for its strengthening of the regulation of private and voluntary provision and its extension of regulation to services for children up to the age of eight (Cohen, 1990). It was also innovating in its aspirations to use regulation to promote the quality of provision; its recognition of ethnic diversity; its emphasis of more co-operation between social services departments, other departments, voluntary organizations and parents; as well as its introduction of the review function for local authorities (Bull *et al.*, 1994). Rather than presenting a snapshot view of services, the review was intended to be used as an ongoing planning tool for a more co-ordinated development strategy for early childhood services (Ceasar *et al.*, 1996).

The Act was still deficient in several important aspects. It imposed limitations upon the extent of regulation — an age limit of eight years old (although not a concern of this study); the exclusion of residential holiday care; the exclusion of care provided by shared nannies employed by up to two sets of parents; the continuing exemption of hospital nurseries; as well as the exclusion of informal care givers (Cohen, 1990). These limitations restricted the protection granted to parents and children. Despite the increased regulation and support responsibilities laid down for local authorities, there was no additional financial resources for them to improve their services. By focusing only on the aspect of care, the Act reaffirmed the perspective that 'care' and 'education' for young children were two distinct phenomena legally, administratively and conceptually (also see Bull *et al.*, 1994). Also, the Act continued to restrict the statutory duties of local authorities to making provision for children and families 'in need', leaving the responsibility for arranging and financing childcare to individual families.

As we have seen, after the adverse developments during the 1980s, there were clearly many more official efforts directed at the issue of childcare provision at the end of the decade. New policy initiatives were centred around several themes: to improve the regulation of the independent sector; to enhance the coordination of different types of provision; to support the independent sector; to encourage employer provision of childcare; to improve the quality of provision; to assist in the provision of after school care and holiday play schemes; and to make provision for those 'in need'. None of the policy initiatives tackled the fundamental problem of insufficient financial resources for the expansion of provision. Indeed, none of the initiatives aimed to expand provision in the public sector. New policy initiatives continued to consider care and education for young children as two separate issues. On the care front, they maintained the view that public provision was only for children and families that were 'in need'.

As in earlier decades, the Government's policy was constrained by the ideological belief that the best place for young children was at home with their parents (mothers in particular). The Government would not encourage mothers to go out to work through the provision of public childcare. As government officials commented,

> Our view is that it is for parents that go out to work to decide how best to care for their children. If they want to or need help in this they should make the appropriate arrangements and meet the costs (Edwina Currie, *Hansard*, 12 July 1988).

> If you have to work you do and if you have to find childcare you find it. When I say 'have' I mean if you really want to (Angela Rumbold, *Family Policy Bulletin*, March 1991, quoted in Cohen and Fraser, 1991, p. 9).

Mrs. Thatcher herself dismissed the need for a national childcare provision. She said that a national provision could lead to 'a whole generation of crèche children ... (who) never understood the security of home' (*The Guardian*, 18 May 1990, quoted in Ginsburg, 1992, p. 173). The then Chancellor of the Exchequer John Major also argued that 'it is not for the government to encourage or discourage women with children from going out to work' (quoted in Ginsburg, 1992, p. 173).

As a consequence of this government policy, the number of local authority day nursery places (publicly-funded daycare) in England actually decreased from 28,437 in 1980 to 27,978 in 1990 (Table 3.1). The decrease should be considered in the context of the increasing use of childminders and playgroups by local authorities to fulfil their statutory duties (DoH, 1989). Nevertheless, the reluctance to develop the public sector encouraged a significant expansion of the independent sector, continuing the developments made in the 1960s and 1970s. As shown in Table 3.1, the number of places for children under five in private nurseries increased 170 per cent from 1980 to 1990. The number of places with childminders increased by 109 per cent. Places with playgroups increased by 13 per cent.

Educational provision in schools grew modestly during the period (see Table 3.1). The growth involved a disproportionate increase in part-time places and a large number of 'rising-fives' going into reception classes. Part-time places with LEA-maintained nursery schools increased 20 per cent from 1980 to 1990. This was against a decrease of 26 per cent in full-time places. For nursery classes and reception classes in maintained primary schools, full-time places increased 20 per cent whereas part-time places increased 67 per cent. In the independent sector, in line with the general growth, full-time places in independent schools increased 30 per

Table 3.1 Childcare Places in England: a Comparison between 1980 and 1990

Premises	Full-time/ Part-time	1980	1990	Percentage change
Public day nurseries		28,437	27,978	-2
Private day nurseries		22,017	59,473	+170
Childminders		98,495	205,567	+109
Playgroups		367,868	416,381	+13
Maintained nursery schools	Full-time	14,079	10,429	-26
	Part-time	34,377	41,096	+20
Reception and nursery classes	Full-time	230,342	275,183	+20
	Part-time	150,122	250,513	+67
Independent schools	Full-time	18,910	24,639	+30
	Part-time	10,832	18,910	+75

Sources: DoH, 1989; DoH, 1996; *Hansard*, 18 April 1995.

cent and part-time places increased 75 per cent.

The Major Period

Mrs. Thatcher fell from power in November 1990. The heightened official attention to the childcare issue at the end of her governance continued in the period when John Major became the Prime Minister. Mr. Major himself showed more sympathy for the issue of childcare as well as for women's employment opportunities.[9] Whereas there were no female ministers in Mrs. Thatcher's Cabinet, he appointed two women to Cabinet posts after the April 1992 General Election. He also gave public support to Opportunity 2000, an employers' initiative to boost women's employment prospects. Meanwhile, the number of women in employment and the number of families headed by a lone parent, usually a lone mother, continued to increase. Recession soon muted the labour shortage worry and the demographic time-bomb was defused by 1992. However, the loose coalition of interests the issue mobilized, and the arguments for working mothers' needs, persisted. The issue of childcare continued to draw the attention of officials. After the appointment of Gillian Shephard as Secretary of State for Employment in 1992, the Department of Employment gradually developed its own agenda for childcare. This was alongside the policy developments carried out by other government departments that also had responsibilities related to childcare. A number of policy initiatives were developed and much more public funding was made available. The major initiatives included the establishment of the framework of training for childcare workers, the Out-of-School Childcare Initiative, the Childcare Disregard, help for the development of childcare in rural areas, and encouragement for the development of the independent sector. This last category included the Nursery Education Voucher Scheme.

The Department of Employment launched the National Vocational Qualifications (NVQ) in Childcare and Education, as well as Playwork, in 1992. This followed from the research project, Working with Under Sevens, mentioned previously. The project was established in May 1989 to prepare recommendations for new forms of national vocational qualifications in childcare. The establishment of the qualification framework represented greater official appreciation of the importance of the quality of provision for young children, and the importance of skilled childcare workers in ensuring quality. The NVQ in Childcare and Education was progressive in recognizing that care and education for young children was inseparable. The Playwork NVQ provided an opportunity to give national recognition and status to playworkers. Besides NVQ, there was also the establishment of Modern Apprenticeships in Childcare. These covered specific skills required for a wide range of childcare and educational settings, equal opportunities in the childcare and education environment, and other core skills. At the end of June 1996, over 6,000 certificates had been awarded for NVQ and over 620 for Modern Apprentices (DfEE, 1996e).

The Department of Employment introduced the Out-of-School Childcare Initiative in 1993. The aim of the initiative was to 'facilitate increased labour market participation, among those who wish to combine work with family life, by parents of school-aged children' (O'Brien and Dench, 1996, p. vii). The official argument was that 'women with school age children are, in principle, more likely to want to increase their labour market participation'. Therefore, the Government saw 'school age childcare as the priority for action' (DfEE, 1996e, p. 23). This argument reflected the influence of the ideology of motherhood, which believed the best place for young children was at home with their mothers. So logically, school age children did not need to stay with their mothers as much as pre-school children. Hence, women with school age children should receive more public help to go back to work. Funding was made available to create after-school and holiday places. It was to cover the initial capital costs and support the operating costs for a maximum of one year. The money was managed and delivered by the Training and Enterprise Councils (TECs) in England and in Wales, and the Scottish Local Enterprise Companies. By the end of March 1996, 71,500 after-school and holiday places for school age children were created. In view of the success of the Initiative, the Government allocated a further grant of 18.9 million pounds for a further three years. This constituted a total investment of nearly 64 million pounds (DfEE, 1996e, p. 12).

To help lone mothers as well as low families, the Government introduced the Childcare Disregard on Family Credit (and other benefits) in the 1993 budget. The idea was originally developed by the Daycare Trust. It was taken up by the Department of Social Security to encourage parents from low income families and with childcare responsibilities to go to work. A major group of these would be lone mothers. While the number of lone mothers had been continually rising, the proportion of those with dependent children and in paid employment had declined, from 47 per cent in 1979 to 41 per cent in 1993 (O'Brien and Dench, 1996). From October 1994, help with childcare[10] charges of up to 40 pounds per week (increased to 60 pounds from April 1996) was made available to families receiving Family Credit, Disability Working Allowance, Housing Benefit or Council Tax Benefit. The scheme applied where charges were incurred for a child under eleven who was cared for by a registered childminder, play scheme or day nursery. Childcare charges were offset against earnings when benefit entitlement was calculated. In connection with this, the number of hours a person was required to work in order to be eligible for Family Credit was reduced to 16 hours. This helped to ensure that parents, particularly lone mothers, could be better off in work even if they were unable to work full-time due to childcare commitments. The government figures in 1996 suggested that 25,000 families were receiving help with childcare charges. Among these 23,000 families were claiming Family Credit, of which 95 per cent were lone parents (DfEE, 1996e, pp. 16, 21).

The introduction of the Childcare Disregard should be considered as generous and progressive in terms of providing financial help for childcare. However, while it was mainly concerned with the aspect of care, it only benefited a limited number of families — families that could be considered as 'disadvantaged' and hence needed help. This policy initiative restated the principle that public help for the care of young children was only for families that were 'in need'. For other families, looking after children was their own private matter. Also, it should be noted that as public provision did not incur charges, the public help made available in effect benefited the independent sector.

The policy principle of providing care for the disadvantaged was also reflected in the policy initiatives aimed at helping rural areas. The White Papers *'Rural England: A Nation Committed to a Living Countryside'* (October, 1995) and *'A Rural White Paper: A Working Countryside for Wales'* (March, 1995) drew attention to the particular problems in rural areas. They noted that childcare[11] provision was too scarce and problems of access were exacerbated by scant public transport. The Rural Development Commission was then established to carry out research and to give advice on rural childcare policy and practice. Four national demonstration rural childcare projects were established through the Commission's Rural Childcare Initiative. The Commission also gave support to rural projects of national voluntary organizations. One example was the new partnership between the National Council of Voluntary Childcare Organizations and Action with Communities in Rural England. The Commission offered further support for local rural childcare projects through its Rural Development Programme. This operated in designated rural areas experiencing the worst concentrations of economic and social problems. In addition, a consortium of Rural TECs was set up for a rural childcare enterprise project, 'Childcare to Careers'. It provided a modularized flexible training route to NVQ level 3 for people wishing to establish childcare facilities in rural areas (DfEE, 1996e, p. 14).

While providing help for deprived families and deprived areas, other policy initiatives during this period sought to encourage 'partnership' between the public sector and the private or voluntary sectors. They in effect encouraged the further expansion of the independent sector in providing childcare. In Wales, a new Under-Fives Initiative was announced in 1995. It was composed of 6 - 7 'Childcare Demonstration' projects. It was set up following 'consultation which had identified the availability of childcare as a crucial factor in helping women return to the labour market' (Ibid., p. 12). Its aim was to 'demonstrate to employers the significant benefits for them of forming partnerships to develop childcare provision for pre-school age children' of their employees. It planned to create 200 places each year in partnership with employers from 1995-96 to 1997-98, with a limited budget of 0.15 million pounds per year (Ibid., p. 13).

The Single Regeneration Budget was another government initiative that sought to encourage partnership between the public and the private or voluntary sectors. The Budget was a fund to support partnerships which offered coherent strategies to regenerate an area or deal with particular problems in an area. The creation of childcare places was supported as part of a comprehensive package of measures to address the needs of a local area. Nearly 40,000 childcare/childminding places were to be created over seven years from 1996 with the support of the first two rounds of the fund (DfEE, 1996e, p. 15).

The Nursery Education Voucher Scheme was introduced towards the end of the Major period. It also aimed to further the development of the independent sector. Vouchers to the value of 1,100 pounds were distributed to parents of every four-year-old to be used in exchange for pre-school education in either the public or the independent sector. It was thought that competition between providers for voucher bearing pupils would enable the good providers to thrive whereas the bad ones would be left to decline. The increased demand for places would create a market force to drive up provision. The introduction of the voucher scheme was a restatement of the policy principle of universal educational provision for older pre-school children. The elements which constrained public policy from providing more childcare in the past had considerable influence on the formulation of the scheme. The emergence and development of the voucher scheme will be discussed in detail in the chapters following.

As I have shown, the policy developments at the end of the 1980s continued into the 1990s. The Major Government enacted a series of policy initiatives for childcare. The establishment of a framework of qualifications for childcare workers revealed the Government's emphasis on the quality of provision and the importance of good skills to ensure such quality. The support for out-of-school and holiday care accompanied the official view that women with school age children had priority in receiving public help to increase their participation in the labour market. For pre-school children, there was new help with childcare charges for families receiving social security benefits and for the development of services in rural areas. This additional help was mainly concerned with the aspect of care and it reflected the historical prioritizing of those 'in need'. For others, the policy principle that caring for young children was their own responsibility remained. Official effort sought to encourage partnerships between the public sector and the private and voluntary sectors. This in effect encouraged the further expansion of the independent sector. Expansion of this sector was one of the aims of the Nursery Education Voucher Scheme. In addition, this scheme showed a revision of official intention to provide universal education for older pre-school children.

With the development of the initiatives mentioned above, during the period of the Major Government, the number of places (see Table 3.2) provided by local authority day nurseries changed from 28,000 in 1990 to 20,200 in 1997, a decrease of 27.9 per cent. The decrease may be explained by the fact that many local authorities gradually provided

Table 3.2 Daycare Places in England: a Comparison between 1990 and 1997

	1990*	1997*	% change
Local authority day nurseries	28,000	20,200	-27.9
Private day nurseries	59,500	173,700	+191.9
Childminders	205,600	365,200	+77.6

*Figures have been rounded to the nearest 100.

Source: DfEE, 1999.

Table 3.3 Provision of Education for Under-Fives in Maintained Nursery and Primary Schools in England: a Comparison between 1990 and 1997

	Nursery schools		Nursery classes		Reception classes	
	Full-time	Part-time	Full-time	Part-time	Full-time	Part-time
1990	10,429	41,096	27,933	227,516	247,250	22,997
1997	8,525	42,209	30,121	286,548	317,052	29,054
% change	-18.3	+2.7	+7.8	+28.7	+28.2	+26.3

Source: DfEE, 1998.

services to children under five in family centres rather than through day nurseries (DoH, 1996). The insufficient provision in the public sector and the demand for childcare facilities drove a further expansion of independent provision. The number of places in private nurseries increased 191.9 per cent, from 59,500 in 1990 to 173,700 in 1997. The number of places with childminders increased from 205,600 in 1990 to 365,200 in 1997, a growth of 77.6 per cent. The growth could be explained partly by the re-registration process introduced under the Children Act 1989 and the new requirement to register places for five- to seven-year-olds. The number of childminding places for children aged under five should be less than the figures provided (DoH, 1996). The number of places with out-of-school clubs and holiday play schemes also expanded significantly, with the help of the Out-of-School Childcare Initiative (Ibid.).

With regard to the level of educational provision, the number of three- and four-year-olds in LEA-maintained nursery schools, nursery classes and reception classes in primary schools increased overall (Table 3.3). Again, as in the previous decade, most of the increases were in part-time places or reception classes. The number of playgroups decreased, from 17,789 in 1990 to 15,800 in 1997, a decrease of 11.2 per cent (DoH, 1998).

Policy under New Labour

At the time of writing the Labour Party is in government. Many of their policies are on-going. Nevertheless, they seem to have taken a more favourable attitude towards childcare provision. They appear to be less constrained by the ideology of motherhood and more sympathetic to women and employment. They are more willing to spend public money on childcare provision and are spending a considerable amount of money to develop childcare services. They launched in May 1998 the National Childcare Strategy which was the first ever comprehensive attempt by any British Government to bring quality, affordable and accessible childcare to children aged 0 to 14 and their families.[12] However, the Labour Government's policy has followed some major trends of previous governments in the development of childcare.[13]

The Labour Government has continued the effort to provide part-time pre-school education for three- and four-year-olds. Soon after their election victory in May 1997, they abolished the voucher scheme. However, they adopted the funding arrangements of the scheme — 1,100 pounds per child per year, and its aim of providing part-time pre-school education for all four-year-olds. This aim was basically achieved by September 1998. A target was then set to provide 66 per cent of three-year-olds with free part-time pre-school education by 2002.

The Labour Government has also continued the trend of public-private partnership and has supported the development of the independent sector as important providers of childcare. After they replaced the voucher scheme, they established the Early Years Development Partnerships, which later became the Early Years Development and Childcare Partnerships (EYDCPs). These are local forums facilitated by local authorities and funded by the Government to develop integrated early years education and care to meet local needs using funding from the Government and other sources. The forums have representation from all local interested parties including providers from the public and the independent sectors.

The Labour Government again see out-of-school childcare as the priority for action. 300 million pounds have been made available through the New Opportunities Fund, a Lottery distribution body, to create new places and to develop integrated care and education schemes for out-of-school childcare. The Fund provides for start up costs and capital for providers in both the independent sector and the public sector.

Other policy initiatives on the care front continue to offer help to those who are disadvantaged and 'in need'. 452 million pounds have been made available through 'Sure Start', a cross-departmental programme for children under four years-old and their families in areas of disadvantage. The programme aims to transform opportunities for young children through better access to childcare, health, early education and support for families. The EYDCPs are involved in the development of Sure Start projects. Another 800 million pounds have been made available through the New Deal for Communities to improve job prospects and the delivery of local services, including childcare, in neighbourhoods with the highest levels of deprivation. The Single Regeneration Budget from the previous government has continued to provide financial resources to support regeneration carried out by local partnerships, including the creation of childcare places. The Childcare Tax Credit was introduced as part of the Working Families Tax Credit, replacing Family Credit from October 1999. Low income families working more than 16 hours a week can receive up to 70 per cent of eligible childcare costs up to maximum cost of 100 pounds for one child and 150 pounds for two or more children. Finally, lone parents who enter the New Deal for Lone Parents programme can receive help with childcare while searching for work or training for work. Up to 100 pounds per week can be paid to contribute to childcare costs at the discretion of Lone Parent Advisers.

The Labour Government's policy initiatives and the funding arrangements for childcare could potentially make a great deal of difference to many young children and their parents. However, the problems resulting from a century's under-development in childcare provision are unlikely to be resolved in a year or two. Whereas the provision for four-year-olds, which is gradually being extended to three-year-olds, is mainly educational and part-time, there is a shortage of public daycare provision, especially for children under three years-old. Most of the daycare provision is in the independent sector which incurs charges. Although financial help is made available through the Childcare Tax Credit, non-working parents including students, parents working less than 16 hours, low income families unable to pay at least 30 per cent of childcare costs, and medium income families not eligible for the financial help but cannot afford the full cost of childcare, are still missing out.[14]

Conclusion

This chapter reviewed the development of childcare policy and childcare provision in Britain, from the early days at the beginning of the century to the present time. Several recurrent themes appeared in this historical review. These included, the separate consideration given to care and education for the under-fives by successive governments; the influence of the ideology of motherhood and the family on childcare policy; the unwillingness of successive governments to spend public money to develop public childcare; the continual expansion of the independent sector, which was reinforced, in the last two decades, by the ideological belief in the introduction of markets for the provision of public services.

Successive governments considered care and education for the under-fives as two separate issues. This view was established formally through two pieces of legislation in the 1910s, and was clarified in a policy statement immediately after the Second World War. On the care side, the Government made provision for children and families that were 'in need'. For other children and families, it was their own responsibility to arrange and finance childcare. On the education side, it was the desire of the government to make provision for older three- and four-year-olds. This approach to childcare provision was reflected time and time again in the policy initiatives which arose in the succeeding fifty years. Successive governments adopted this policy principle.

Underlying the policy principle mentioned above, was the ideology of motherhood and the traditional family. The closure of childcare facilities after the Second World War is an example of the effect this ideological belief had on policy. The Thatcher Government reinforced this view by suggesting that childcare was essentially a private family matter and actively discouraged public provision. When the changed socioeconomic situation drew the government's attention to the childcare issue towards the end of the 1980s, this ideological belief prevented any real efforts to expand public provision. It was the same ideology that, in the 1990s, led to the prioritization of out-of-school childcare for school age children.

The development of childcare policy, in terms of providing more public childcare, was hindered by the belief in the need to control public spending. As a result, little or insufficient public money was made available to develop provision. In the early 1970s, plans to develop provision were hit by the in-coming Labour Government who introduced severe cut backs to public expenditure. The Thatcher Government continued to enact policies to reduce public spending and actively discouraged the use of public funding to expand childcare provision. Towards the end of the 1980s, increased official efforts for childcare failed to address the problem of insufficient financial resources for the expansion of provision. More public money was made available in the 1990s. However, the new money was prioritized for those 'in need' and for the provision of pre-school education for older pre-school children. A lot of this money was used to fund provision in the independent sector.

The insufficient provision in the public sector and the demand for childcare facilities triggered a continual expansion of the independent sector. Childminding and playgroups developed significantly in the 1960s and 1970s. They were supported by successive Governments as alternative forms of provision to public daycare and nursery education. In the 1980s and the 1990s, government's support for the independent sector was reinforced by the ideological belief in the development of markets for the provision of public services. Public money was used to help the further expansion of the independent sector. Independent provision, particularly private nurseries and childminding, grew extensively during the period.

The issues summarized here all had an important impact on the form of the voucher scheme. How these issues affected the scheme will be discussed in full in the following chapters.

Notes

1   For the earliest childcare provision, also see Ruggie, 1984, chapter 5; Cohen and Fraser, 1991.
2   For developments in the public sector in the 1960s and 1970s, also see Randall, 1995.
3   According to information provided by the NCMA.
4   The organisation changed its name to Pre-school Learning Alliance (PLA) in 1995 in order to emphasize the educational value of the provision.
5   Information concerning the establishment and early development of the PPA (PLA as it is known now) is supplied by the PLA.
6   Also see Randall, 1995; Cohen, 1990.
7   Data quoted in Randall, 1995, p. 335.
8   It should be noted that the government's use of the word 'childcare' referred mainly to the element of care. It usually did not involve, or only very marginally involved, the element of education.
9   Also see Randall, 1996.
10   Again, 'childcare' here mainly involved the element of care. Also see note 8.
11   See note 10.
12   Daycare Trust (1999c), 'What is the National Childcare Strategy?', Briefing Paper, *Childcare Now* (special issue), May 1999, Daycare Trust, London.

13   For the Labour Government's new policy initiatives and funding arrangements for childcare, also see Daycare Trust (1999b), 'The National Childcare Strategy', *Childcare Now*, May 1999.
14   Daycare Trust (1999a), 'Childcare Gaps', *Childcare Now*, May 1999.

4 Agenda Setting, Option Selection and Legislation

After reviewing the development of childcare policy and childcare provision, this chapter and the two subsequent chapters look in detail at the policy process of the Nursery Education Voucher Scheme. As set out in chapter 2, I consider that there are two dimensions in the analysis of the policy process — the 'actors' and the 'process'. The dynamic 'process' of policy making is separated into some distinct but highly related stages. Each of the stages has a unique function in the policy process and distinct implications for policy outcomes. Each of them requires separate and independent analysis.

I identified six policy stages for the voucher scheme. This chapter examines the first three stages of agenda setting, option selection and legislation. In the stage of 'agenda setting', the provision of pre-school education for four-year-olds reached the Government's policy agenda. A provision that would involve the aspect of care, or would include younger children, failed to become the focus of government action. In the stage of 'option selection', a universal voucher scheme was chosen from several other options to make the provision. Public funding was made available through vouchers which were given to parents of every eligible child to exchange for part-time pre-school education. No money was made available specifically to create new places. In the 'legislation' stage, the Opposition, some Conservative MPs and the peers lobbied against the voucher proposal. However, ministers successfully pressed the legislation necessary for nationwide implementation of the voucher scheme through Parliament.

Involved in the analysis of each policy stage is the dimension of the actors. As explained in chapter 2, this dimension is concerned with the activities of policy actors — individuals, political institutions or interest organizations, who attempt to influence policy decision making. The analysis will seek to identify these actors and their actions and decisions. It will also look at the ways in which these actions and decisions are affected by previous policy, the rules of actors, and the resource relationships between actors. The purpose of the discussion is to identify the crucial factors that have influenced the development of the policy initiative. The discussion will also consider the relevance of the theoretical stances of Marxism, pluralism and state autonomy to the empirical situation.

Pre-school Education as a Policy Agenda

Policy agenda, as defined by Kingdon, refers to 'the list of subjects or problems to which government officials and people outside of government closely associated with those officials, are paying some serious attention at any given time' (Kingdon, 1984, p. 3). Among the set of all conceivable issues or problems, as Walt has stated, 'some get attended to seriously in preference to others'. The process of agenda setting 'narrows down the set of possible subjects to those that actually become the focus of attention' (Walt, 1994, p. 53). As discussed in chapter 3, a number of socioeconomic factors in the 1980s led to heightened official attention to the childcare issue. By the beginning of the 1990s, a major policy initiative to expand provision was under discussion. However, part-time pre-school education for four-year-olds became the focus of government action. Neither a provision of care or a combination of care and education, nor a provision that would include younger children, was on the policy agenda. Such a policy would do little to help mothers of young children to take up employment. The neglect of the caring aspect and exclusion of children younger than four raises important questions. Why did pre-school education receive so much attention in preference to a provision that involved the element of care? Why was the provision only for four-year-olds? What were the crucial factors that shaped the decisions?

Kingdon (1984) has suggested a three-stream approach to explain how issues reach government policy agenda. The three streams are the problem stream, the politics stream and the policy stream. An issue is taken seriously by the government only when a major opportunity opens up in each of these three streams. That is when, in the problem stream, officials define an existing condition as a problem and consider that something needs to be changed; in the politics stream, visible and hidden participants — organized interests, politicians, government officials, specialists, etc., press the issue onto the policy agenda; in the policy stream, policy actors select, based on a number of criteria, from among the problems and the alternative policy solutions the proposals which will become public policy. This approach is useful for explaining why childcare provision received serious official attention in the 1990s and why the provision of pre-school education for four-year-olds alone was on the policy agenda. Opportunities had opened up in all the three streams for this form of provision, but not for a provision that would involve the element of care or include younger children.

In the problem stream, officials had come to recognize the lack of childcare provision as a problem. The demand for childcare facilities had increased significantly during the 1980s (also see chapter 3). The number of employed women with young children had increased. The rate of labour market participation by these women grew from 24 per cent in 1983 to 41 per cent in 1989. The percentage of families headed by a single parent had also increased. The rate was 17 per cent in 1989, nine out of ten of which were led by a single mother.[1] In addition, there was the concern over the demographic time-bomb. Both the government and employers had to persuade mothers, especially those with badly needed skills, to go back to work by providing more childcare. The insufficient childcare places to meet the increased demand had become a problem.

In the politics stream, interested actors had been pressing the childcare issue onto the policy agenda (also see chapter 3). There was increasing recognition of the importance of childcare provision in aiding women's employment prospects. A series of feminism inspired childcare campaigns were conducted during the 1980s. Childcare interest groups, academics, child-centred professionals, local authority associations and other interested actors persistently called for more government action and more public funding for childcare provision. Both the Liberal Democratic Party and the Labour Party were giving more attention to the issue. In 1985, the Labour Party produced its Charter for the Under-Fives. With the pressure from these various organized interests, the Conservative Party activists were worried that they would loose voters if they continued to ignore the childcare issue.

In the policy stream, government officials looked into the problems and possible solutions and made a decision on what was to become policy. In response to the House of Commons education committee report, *Educational Provision for the Under-Fives*, the Government set up a committee to make further inquiries into the issue (also see chapter 3). The Committee of Inquiry into the Content of the Educational Experience of Under-Fives was established in March 1989, chaired by the minister at the DES, Angela Rumbold. Members of the Committee included eight early years professionals. Their main responsibility was to consider the quality of the educational experience which should be offered to three- and four-year-olds, especially those aspects of the issue highlighted by the House of Commons education committee report. The resulting report, 'Starting with Quality',[2] was published in autumn 1990. It pointed out the urgent need to raise the quality of a good deal of existing provision, including those that were primarily purported to provide care, such as day nurseries. The report recognized the range of different experiences that children would have before they started compulsory schooling. It called for collaboration at various levels and argued that care and education for the under-fives were complementary and inseparable. Although the Committee was centrally concerned with the quality of provision, the report also addressed the issue of quantity. It pointed to the situation of demand outstripping supply and stressed the urgent need to expand quality provision.

At around the same period of time, another government committee had also looked into the issue of under-fives provision. It approached the issue from a different direction, not from the direction of enhancing the educational experience of young children, but from the direction of aiding women's employment opportunities. The Ministerial Group on Women's Issues which had been meeting since 1986, recognized the importance of childcare provision to women's employment prospects. In March 1989, it suggested a five-point programme for developing childcare (see chapter 3). The Group also proposed to provide working women with tax free vouchers which would be redeemable at any nursery. The vouchers would be supplied by employers who would be able to offset the value against taxation. The argument of the committee was that by helping with the cost of childcare, more women would be able to afford to use childcare facilities for their young children. They themselves would then be freed from looking after children to take up employment. The Group urged their proposal be implemented the coming financial year, or at least, for the Prime Minister to include it in a manifesto pledge (*The Independent on Sunday*, 8 July 1990).

The Ministerial Group's proposal, however, was opposed by some actors at the centre of the state. These actors included the Prime Minister, ministers from the Treasury Office and other right-wing Cabinet ministers. They opposed the proposal for two main reasons. First of all, enacting the proposal would be expensive. Such a scheme of childcare vouchers for working mothers in effect involved the provision of daycare for any pre-school child whose mother wanted to take up employment. A large number of mothers would be eligible for vouchers which would be offset against taxation. A scheme on this scale would mean an unquantifiable potential cost to the Treasury. The central state actors, drawing upon the belief in the need to control public spending, rejected the proposal. In particular, the Chancellor of the Exchequer and ministers from his office were strongly opposed to the idea. They used their authority of supervising the tax system to refuse to alter the tax law which would be necessary for implementing such a scheme (Ibid.).

The proposal of childcare vouchers for working mothers was also rejected on the grounds that it was in conflict with the ideology of the right-wing. I argued in chapter 3 that the Thatcher Government's approach to childcare policy was compatible with the New Right Ideology. The New Right thinking argued for social order and authority based on traditional social, religious and moral views. Advocates believed that the family was crucial for maintaining social stability. The family was to be responsible for the economic and moral welfare of its members. The woman in the family was to be a full-time mother socializing the children and caring for the husband. Followers of the New Right Ideology attacked what they saw as the breakdown of the family in modern society, citing the evidence of working mothers, who by taking paid work, failed to put the needs of their children before their own (see Abbott and Wallace, 1992). The proposal of childcare vouchers which had the purpose of aiding women's employment prospects was in stark contradiction to the New Right stance. Many Cabinet ministers in the Conservative Government were distinctly right-wing and believed in the ideology of the family and motherhood. Despite their increased attention to the childcare issue, officials had emphasized that the Government would not expand provision in order to aid mothers to take up employment (see chapter 3). The Prime Minister Margaret Thatcher was herself a supporter of the family. She had commented that a national childcare provision would lead to 'a whole generation of Crèche children ... (who) never understood the security of home' (*The Guardian*, 18 May 1990, also quoted in chapter 3). Therefore, drawing upon the ideology of the family and motherhood, the central state actors rejected the proposal of childcare vouchers for working mothers (*The Guardian*, 9 July 1990).

The state actors who opposed the proposal of childcare vouchers were the leading members of the government. They were situated at the centre of the political state and had control over the resources crucial for the expansion of childcare provision. The Prime Minister had the authority to oversee the work of the government, including what was to be on the policy agenda. Ministers from the Treasury Office had control over public financial resources and had the authority to supervise the tax system. The right-wing ministers had the organisational resources of party-political support since the Conservative Party was generally right-wing and the right-wing ideology was the dominant ideology of the Party. As members of the Cabinet they also had the authority to set the government's policy agenda. Using their resources, these central state actors exercised what Bachrach and Baratz (1970) defined as the 'second face of power' (see chapter 2). They made a nondecision to keep the proposal of childcare vouchers, in effect a proposal that involved the provision of daycare, off the policy agenda. Such a nondecision upheld their own values and beliefs. It sustained the situation whereby women were deprived of the opportunity to participate fully in paid work.

The central state actors had to ensure electoral support and election victory, and had to make some sort of response to social demand. At the Conservative Party Annual Conference in October 1990, the Prime Minister suggested a manifesto commitment to nursery education vouchers instead (*TES*, 21 October 1990). As stated in chapter 3, previous government policy for childcare had considered the provision of care and education for under-fives as two separate issues. The policy had been to provide part-time education for three- and four-year-olds, and to provide care only for those who were 'in need'. However, there had never been enough places to cater for all three- and four-year-olds. While there was a demand for the expansion of childcare provision that involved both aspects of care and education, there was a separate demand for the expansion of educational provision. The latter was expressed within the House of Commons education committee report in 1989. The Report called for the resumption of the objective set out in the 1972 Education White Paper for a universal educational provision for three- and four-year-olds. Therefore, the act of making a manifesto commitment and putting the expansion of nursery education on the policy agenda would ease, to some extent, social and political demand. In addition, historically nursery education was mostly part-time and for three- and four-year-olds only. The provision of daycare, however, was full-time and for children younger than three years-old as well. Making provision for nursery education instead of daycare would cost the Treasury less. Also, it would not contradict the ideology of the right-wing. Since the provision would only be part-time, it would not encourage mothers of young children to go out to work full-time. The Prime Minister's decision was influenced by the belief in the need to control public spending and the ideology of the family and motherhood. It was also influenced by previous childcare policy. The decision ignored the findings of the Rumbold Report that care and education for the under-fives were complementary and inseparable. It also disregarded the demand in society for more childcare provision in order to assist mothers in taking up employment.

After the Conservative Party conference, the Prime Minister asked two right-wing junior ministers to prepare a paper on education vouchers. The Secretary of State for Education, John MacGregor, only gave 'qualified support' to the idea (*TES*, 21 October 1990). Vouchers for education had never been successfully implemented in either the United States or Britain. After looking into the idea, ministers ruled it out as impractical. There was no further government action at that time. It was not until later, when further opportunities opened up in all the three streams, that the provision of pre-school education for four-year-olds re-surfaced on the political agenda.

In the problem stream, the Home Office was alarmed by the emerging cases of juvenile crime. The most serious ones were the Tyneside riots in 1991 and the murder committed by two children in February 1993. Home Office officials were impressed by the long-term beneficial effects of a nursery education project on combating juvenile crime in the United States. They showed interest in developing similar educational provision for young children in the United Kingdom (see Randall, 1996).

In the politics stream, a considerable number of national debates forced the issue of pre-school education onto the policy agenda. During the 1992 General Election campaign, both the Labour Party and the Liberal Democratic Party proclaimed their commitment to a universal provision of nursery education. The Labour Party pledged to achieve this by the year 2000. The Liberal Democrats made it a central plank of their electoral manifesto. They planned that if necessary the provision would be funded by an extra 1p on income tax (Ibid.). In addition, a number of national reports called for a higher commitment to early childhood education. Two most notable ones were from the National Commission on Education and the Royal Society of Arts (see Pugh, 1996). The National Commission on Education was established in 1991 as an independent advisory body. The first of its seven goals was the development of a national strategy for early childhood education. The Commission published the report, *Learning to Succeed*, in 1993. It called for a high-quality publicly-funded education provision for all three- and four-your-olds. The Royal Society of Arts published the report, *Start Right*, in March the following year. It made a similar appeal for a high quality nursery education provision for all children aged three and four.

In the policy stream, policy makers selected from alternative solutions the proposal that would become policy. In December 1993, the Prime Minister John Major announced that the Government intended to work towards the goal of universal nursery education for three- and four-year-olds. Further details of the proposal were being investigated by education ministers. It was speculated that a plan to provide education vouchers to all parents of three- and four-year-olds regardless of income would be unveiled by the education secretary John Patten (*The Sunday Times*, 26 December 1993). There was no sign of a government decision until October 1994. Then, at the Conservative Party Annual Conference, the Prime Minister made a 'cast iron' commitment to the expansion of nursery education before the next General Election. However, the provision was not for three- and four-year-olds as previously stated, but for four-year-olds only. It was to be made not only by nursery schools and classes, but also by reception classes, pre-schools/playgroups and other independent providers. Such a provision was more suitably referred to as 'pre-school education', rather than 'nursery education'.

In January 1994, 91 per cent of all four-year-olds were already in educational provision in schools[3] (*Hansard*, 9 June 1995). The rate was only 45 per cent for three-year-olds (Ibid., 5 July 1995). Making provision for four-year-olds only would significantly minimise the number of extra places that would have to be created. It would thus have a minimal effect on public expenditure. Furthermore, as discussed in chapter 3, previous government policy had been reluctant to develop the public sector. This had given rise to a rapid and continual expansion of the private and voluntary sectors. In January 1994, 19 per cent of four-year-olds were in some form of private or voluntary provision (Ibid., 9 June 1995). The inclusion of voluntary playgroups and private nurseries to make provision for the four-year-olds would further lighten the burden on the government to create extra places. The Prime Minister's decisions were made by drawing upon the rule to minimize public spending. They were also influenced by previous childcare policy and its consequence. However, the decisions deviated from the requests of the campaigners for nursery education,[4] who asked for public provision, i.e. a provision made in LEA-maintained nursery classes or nursery schools, for all three- and four-year-olds.

The provision of pre-school education for four-year-olds was now on the policy agenda. Analytically, neither the theoretical stance of pluralism, Marxism nor state autonomy alone can be used to explain the setting of the policy agenda. It was the result of pluralist politics and the need of the economy that led the Government to pay serious attention to the issue of childcare and consider expanding provision. The demand in society for more childcare facilities as expressed through various organized interest groups, and the response made by opposition political parties to the social demand, had effects. The worry over the demographic time-bomb which meant there was an economic need to get mothers to go back to work in order to meet the projected labour shortage, had effects on the Government too.

Neither the social demand, the political pressure nor the need of the economy, however, had influence on what ultimately became the focus of policy action. The decisions on the provision of pre-school education for four-year-olds were the result of a high degree of autonomy in policy making of the central state actors. They were the leading members of the government and had control over the resources crucial for policy making. They made the respective decisions according to their own policy preferences, ignoring the requests and demands of society actors and other state actors. They ignored the recommendation of the Rumbold Report that care and education for the under-fives were complementary and inseparable. They disregarded the general demand in society for more childcare facilities in order to aid women's employment prospects. In particular, they rejected the proposal of the Ministerial Group on Women's Issues of childcare vouchers for working women which would in effect provide daycare for young children and help mothers to take up employment. Also, the arrangement that the provision of pre-school education was for four-year-olds only and could be made by voluntary playgroups and private nurseries, deviated from the requests of the campaigners for public provision of nursery education, i.e. a provision made in LEA-maintained nursery schools and classes, for all three- and four-year-olds. The autonomy of the central state actors in agenda setting was equivalent to type I* state autonomy (see chapter 2). Their policy preferences diverged from the preferences of other state actors and society actors, and they acted on their own preferences.

The central state actors were thus the most powerful in agenda setting. They set the policy agenda drawing upon their own rules. The major ones here included the belief in the need to control public spending, and the ideology of the family and motherhood. Previous childcare policy, which had considered care and education for the under-fives as two separate issues, and had been reluctant to develop the public sector, had effects on the decisions of the central state actors too. The fact that previous policy had given separate consideration to care and education, and that public childcare provision had been slow to develop, was also due to the influence of the ideology of the family and motherhood, and the belief in the need to control public spending (see chapter 3). These rules of the most powerful actors were reproduced once again with the decision to provide part-time pre-school education for four-year-olds only. With the reproduction of these rules came the reproduction of the social institutions of the traditional family, the gendered division of labour at home and at work, and a set of related constraints which in practice combined to make women lesser citizens (see Pateman, 1989).

Selecting the Voucher Option

After John Major announced his 'cast iron' commitment to the expansion of educational provision for four-year-olds, discussions were held about ways to fulfil the Prime Minister's promise. There were proposals which would aid women's employment prospects. However, from the various options, the Government made the decision to use a universal voucher system, which included vouchers of 1,100 pounds, to make the provision.

Why was this particular form of voucher scheme adopted in preference to other options?

After the Conservative Party conference, a task force was set up under the Secretary of State for Education to consider possible ways of implementing the Prime Minister's promise. Members of the task force included three senior officials in the DFE — an under-secretary, an assistant secretary and a principal officer. The task force carried out inquiries with under-fives groups and other interested actors. It worked closely with other related government departments including the DoH, the Department of Employment, the Home Office and the Department of Trade and Industry. The Office for Standards in Education (Ofsted) was also involved since the new policy initiative was about the provision of education (*TES*, 4 November 1994).

The task force looked into all possible ways of implementing the Prime Minister's promise. One of the options under consideration was a voucher scheme. Vouchers for education was not a new idea (see *The Independent*, 7 May 1995). It was first suggested by Thomas Paine in *The Rights of Man* published in 1792. He argued that the best way to provide free schooling was to give parents the purchasing power to 'buy' education through vouchers. This idea of education vouchers had reappeared at various points in the subsequent 200 years. It was attractive to both the political left and the political right. For the political left, education vouchers would allow parents to use public money to pay for education in private institutions. This would enable poor children to go to private schools. For the political right which advocated the free market economy, vouchers would open up a market for education. Competition between institutions for voucher bearing pupils would promote the good ones and allow them to flourish. The bad ones would be left to wither and die. However, vouchers for education had only ever been implemented on a small scale. They involved a massive bureaucracy and were considered as too expensive and impractical. More recently, in the mid-1980s, the Secretary of State for Education Sir Keith Joseph had considered education vouchers and thought they were 'intellectually attractive' (*The Independent*, 23 March 1995). He was later convinced by officials in his department that they were not practical. In October 1990, as stated previously, the then Prime Minister Margaret Thatcher suggested a manifesto commitment to education vouchers for pre-school children. Again they were later ruled out as impractical.

Education vouchers were being considered again in the mid-1990s by the Major Government. The right-wing think-tanks actively promoted the idea to the government. Two right-wing think tanks — the Centre for Policy Studies (CPS) and the Adam Smith Institute, each recommended a voucher scheme.[5]   The CPS's proposal was published as a pamphlet in December 1994, written by the deputy director.   It argued for a universal voucher scheme of 700 pounds a year.   They were to be given to parents of all four-year-olds to exchange for pre-school education in pre-schools/ playgroups, independent or state schools.   Parents would be free to top up the voucher whose value would be about half the cost of an independent nursery school place.   The pamphlet also called for an immediate halt to local authorities' monopolization of public funding for under-fives provision.   It argued that opening up opportunities to private and voluntary sectors would lower the cost of pre-school education expansion and would ensure parental choice.

The Adam Smith Institute's proposal was set out in the report *Pre-school For All: A Market Solution*, in January 1995.   It was written by David Soskin, a founder of a group of independent nurseries.   It suggested giving parents of all three- and four-year-olds vouchers to cover the cost of childcare through a means-tested voucher system.   Those parents who were paying income tax at 40 per cent would receive a voucher of 1,000 pounds, about 20 per cent of the cost of a nursery place.   Basic-rate taxpayers would be given a voucher of 3,000 pounds.   Others who were below the basic-rate level would receive a full cost voucher of 5,000 pounds.   The report also recommended that the provision should be an integration of care and education.   It should be full-time, from 8 am to 6 pm, and all year round. These arrangements would give those parents who were currently forced to stay at home by the cost of childcare the choice of going out to work.   They would then reduce their dependency on the welfare state.   In agreement with the CPS, the report argued that local authorities should lose their role in under-fives provision and should be replaced by the private sector.

The Adam Smith proposal was more progressive than the CPS scheme by advocating a means-tested voucher system, an integration of care and education, full-time and all year round provision for all three- and four-year-olds.   This proposal was very similar to the childcare vouchers for working mothers previously recommended by the Ministerial Group for Women's Issues, although the latter would have provided for children younger than three as well.   Like the Ministerial Group's proposal, however, such a scheme would be expensive.   It also had the aim of assisting parents who currently had to stay at home to look after young children (mostly mothers), to go out to work.

Ministers who were distinctly right-wing supported the idea of a voucher scheme in principle.   They thought that in creating a market for under-fives provision, competition between providers for voucher bearing pupils would allow good providers to thrive while the bad ones would fare less successfully.   The increased demand for places would create a market force to drive up provision. A voucher scheme would then enhance parental choice, in terms of both quality and quantity. When it came to choosing between the means-tested voucher system proposed by the Adam Smith Institute and the universal voucher scheme recommended by the CPS, ministers gave their support to the CPS proposal. The CPS proposal was cheaper. It would not encourage mothers to go out to work full-time. The rules these central state actors followed, were the ones to control public spending and enhance the traditional family and motherhood. The Prime Minister also favoured a universal voucher system for the reason that it would be a potential vote-winner. The rule he followed was one to protect and promote the interests of his party by ensuring electoral support and election victory. He thought that the giving to parents of every four-year-old a voucher would be favoured by both the middle class and the less well-off electorate.

A social policy conference on funding pre-school education was organized by the CPS on 15 March 1995. Ministers and civil servants from the Treasury Office and DFE attended the conference. Supporters of a universal voucher scheme were also present. The Chief Secretary to the Treasury, who was a supporter of right-wing thinking, opened the conference. He outlined the possible ways of implementing the Prime Minister's promise to provide pre-school education for all four-year-olds. He saw a voucher scheme had 'powerful attractions' with a bidding system (to be explained later) as the main alternative. He was careful not to prejudice the outcome of the DFE inquiry being conducted under the Secretary of State for Education. However, his hinted preference for a universal voucher system, such as the one proposed by the CPS, was clear.[6]

Both right-wing think-tanks, the CPS and the Adam Smith Institute, should be seen as insiders to the Conservative Government. However, a nondecision was made and the second face of power was used to keep the Adam Smith plan — a proposal which would challenge the rules of the most powerful leading members of the government, out of the discussion. Although the leading members of the government favoured the CPS's proposal, the CPS was not more influential than the Adam Smith Institute in policy decision making. No resource exchange had taken place between the CPS and the Government. It was simply because the preference of the CPS was similar to that of the leading members of the government who in effect acted on their own preference.

The majority of other interest groups were not fond of the voucher option. During the DFE inquiry, the DFE task force met or visited more than 90 organizations and institutions, including providers for under-fives. It also received written submissions from more than 70 organizations.[7] The concept of a voucher scheme was among the wide range of issues discussed by interested actors. However, only written responses from four organizations supported the idea (*Hansard*, 14 June 1995). The discussion paper 'Vouchers and Early Years Provision', prepared by the AMA for the Early Childhood Education Forum (ECEF),[8] summarized interested organizations' concerns (AMA, September 1994).

The paper argued that, firstly, the range of current provision would 'not lend itself easily to a set of definable characteristics for which vouchers can be used' (p. 1). Each type of provision, and indeed each individual service, had a different unit cost. The inclusion of a cost threshold by a voucher system would risk the effect of driving down costs to a lowest common denominator. This would call into question the viability of any intended expansion. Secondly, while vouchers would essentially provide support for running costs, they would not 'on their own put in place any supporting infrastructure', nor would they 'take account of the start-up costs of new institutions, or the cost of adapting/expanding existing ones'. Thirdly, the administration of such a scheme 'would inevitably lead to an increase in absolute bureaucracy and add complexity to overall funding mechanisms' (p. 3). Fourthly, how the voucher system was going to define the eligibility of providers might have an effect on promoting specific types of provision. In addition, existing voucher schemes had produced no evidence that they had encouraged an increase in provision. It could not be assumed that entitlement to vouchers would enhance either parental choice or the levels of provision.

Several other criticisms were levelled at the voucher scheme from interest organizations. Under a universal voucher system, those children who were currently in LEA-maintained settings would continue having their pre-school education free. Parents who were already paying for nursery places would get the same provision free or partly paid, depending on the value of the voucher. For a scheme such as the one proposed by the CPS, the voucher would only cover about half of the cost of a private pre-school education place. While subsidizing the well-off, it would not provide sufficient help for the most needy. After all, without money to create new places, four-year-olds in areas where there were not enough places would still not receive pre-school education. Therefore, a universal voucher scheme was more likely to lead to 'increased public expenditure to fund no net increase in provision', and 'the transfer of public subsidy from the poor to the rich' (AMA, September 1994, p. 2). The rule of these interest organizations was one to expand provision for the under-fives in a cost effective way. They did not prefer the voucher option which would not achieve that purpose. However, these interest organizations did not have access to the resources that the Government would need in this stage of option selection. They were unable to intervene in the government's decision, whatever that might be. They could only express their views through the official consultation exercise and other means such as the publication of discussion papers or press releases. They had no direct involvement and no real influence on the choosing of the policy option.

The Secretary of State for Education and officials in her department, including members of the task force, were not fond of a voucher scheme either. Under a voucher scheme, funding would be made available through vouchers and there would be no money specifically for the creation of new places. As a result, it was very unlikely that there would be a significant expansion in provision. Speaking at the same CPS conference, a minister from the DFE warned that if there were not enough places for every four-year-old with a voucher (currently there were not), 'the virtues and joys of a voucher scheme will not be forthcoming' (*TES*, 7 April 1995).[9] Speaking in an interview with the Times Educational Supplement (TES), the Secretary of State for Education also argued that vouchers were 'not the favoured option' (*TES*, 7 April 1995). She feared that there would be an angry political backlash if the vouchers were distributed but parents in some areas were unable to use them due to the unavailability of places (*The Daily Mail*, 2 May 1995). The consideration of the DFE was more practical in nature. The rule they drew upon was one to achieve the aim of expanding pre-school education provision. They did not favour the voucher option because they did not think that it would fulfil the purpose. They preferred instead a bidding system. Under a bidding system, independent providers and local authority schools would bid for funding for the expansion of pre-school places from the DFE or a new funding agency. The DFE believed that such a system would be more likely to expand provision, especially in areas where there was a shortage of places. It would also be speedier because legislation would not be required whereas a nationwide voucher scheme would require legislation (*The Sunday Telegraph*, 19 March 1995).

The DFE, however, were not influential in making the policy decision. Those who had influence were those who preferred the option of a universal voucher system. These actors included the Prime Minister, ministers from the Treasury Office and other right-wing ministers. They were situated at the centre of the political system and enjoyed prominent positions in political networks. They had control over the resources that were crucial for any policy development. The Prime Minister had the authority in appointing Cabinet members. He in effect over-saw the work of every Cabinet member and every government department. Ministers from the Treasury had control over public financial resources. The right-wing ministers had the organisational resources of party-political support, since the right-wing ideology was the dominant ideology of the

Conservative Party at that time. DFE ministers and civil servants had to depend on the financial resources controlled by the Treasury for any form of expansion in provision. They had to depend on the authority of the Prime Minister to give any policy initiative the go-ahead. This, in turn, was reliant upon the support of other members of the Conservative Party, particularly the MPs.

With their crucial resources, the leading members of the government exercised power over the DFE task force. They brought about a change in the latter's policy preference. By the end of April, the DFE agreed that a voucher scheme would go ahead, but with conditions. There would be a full-scale campaign by DFE officials to ensure the availability of enough places before introducing a voucher scheme. This was what they called the 'two-stage plan'. In the first stage, a bidding system would be set up and run privately by a quango or by the DFE to create new nursery places across the country. Once an adequate number of places were created, the second stage, a voucher scheme, would be introduced.[10]

Right-wing ministers again opposed this proposal. They did not like the idea of a bidding system in the first instance. They considered that a bidding system would give too much power to the central government and local authority officials. This would be unfavourable to private and voluntary institutions, and thus unfavourable to the development of a market for pre-school education provision (*The Times*, 14 June 1995). There was no agreement and a decision could still not be made. Time was running short because the Prime Minister promised to expand pre-school education before the next General Election. Supporters of the voucher scheme exercised further power over the DFE and brought a further change in the latter's policy preference. The DFE eventually agreed to a universal voucher scheme (*The Daily Mail*, 22 May 1995).

On 6 July 1995, the Secretary of State for Education announced the policy relating to the pre-school education voucher scheme in the House of Commons (*Hansard*, 6 July 1995). Parents of every four-year-old would be given a voucher of 1,100 pounds to exchange for a year (three terms) of pre-school education. This would mostly be a part-time provision (apart from reception classes in state schools which would be full-time) — 2.5 hours a session and five sessions a week. The provision could be made by any private, voluntary or public institution. Institutions which would accept the vouchers would have to make a commitment to offer education compatible with a set of desirable learning outcomes for children's learning. They also would have to agree to be inspected. The School Curriculum and Assessment Authority (SCAA) would be consulting on the desirable learning outcomes. The DoH and the DFE would be consulting on inspection arrangements. The issue and redemption of vouchers would be undertaken by a private company under contract. Total expenditure of the scheme in England would be 730 million pounds. It would be funded by 185 million pounds of new money (of which 20 million pounds would be for administration and inspection) and 545 million pounds recouped from current government funding for LEAs under-fives provision. The scheme would be phased in. Phase One would be voluntarily starting in some local authority areas from April 1996. In Phase Two, the voucher scheme would be implemented nationwide from April 1997.

A universal voucher scheme was chosen from other options (a means-tested voucher scheme, a bidding system and a two-stage plan) to implement the Prime Minister's promise to expand pre-school education for all four-year-olds. To sum up, this result of policy decision making was due to, firstly, the supporters of a universal voucher scheme being more powerful than other actors. These supporters included the leading members of the government. They were situated at the centre of the state and had the resources that were crucial for any policy development. Secondly, these central state actors' preference for a universal voucher scheme was influenced by the right-wing ideology to create markets for the provision of public services; the ideological belief of enhancing the traditional family and motherhood; the belief in the need to control public expenditure; and the view that a universal voucher system would win electoral support. The recommendation of a means-tested voucher scheme to provide full-time care and education by the Adam Smith Institute would have aided mothers' employment opportunities. However, a nondecision was made so that the proposal was kept out of the debate. Here, the second face of power was involved to marginalize a policy option which challenged the rules of the most powerful actors.

The theoretical stance of state autonomy is the most suitable to explain the nature of the state in the context of this policy stage of option selection. The central state actors enjoyed a high degree of autonomy in choosing the policy option of a universal voucher scheme. They were able to act on their own policy preference ignoring the preferences of other state actors and society actors. The autonomy they enjoyed was equivalent to type I* state autonomy when they acted on their policy preference despite opposition from interest organizations in society. Their autonomy was equivalent to type II* state autonomy when they, repeatedly, intervened in the decisions of the DFE (task force) and brought about changes to the latter's policy preferences. Their autonomy was equivalent to type III* state autonomy when their policy preference was non-divergent from the preference of the CPS and they, in effect, went on to act on their own preference.

Legislation and Parliament

Some months after the announcement of the voucher scheme, the legislative process started in Parliament. Phase One of the voucher scheme did not require legislation. The Government had the authority to try out new policy initiatives. In Phase Two, legislation was required to create a legal basis for the scheme to be implemented nationwide. Parliament is conventionally the top decision making body of a country which adopts a democratic representative political system. As stated in Chapter 2, the model of representative democracy is especially influential in Britain because of the constitutional importance of Parliament. Parliament is the sole law-giving body. Its power is constrained only by convention not by constitution. However, some scholars have argued that in reality, the influence of Parliament on policy making is insignificant and its role in the policy process is marginal (see Walt, 1994). What was the significance of Parliament in the policy process of the voucher scheme? Did the central state actors also dominate in this democratic institution and have autonomy in legislating?

Ministers started to prepare for legislation at the end of 1995. Apart from the voucher scheme, there was another piece of legislation concerning education that the Government wanted to introduce before the next General Election. This was concerned with making opting out more attractive for schools by allowing grant-maintained (GM) schools to borrow money against their assets. Measures were also planned to create a fast track to GM status for church schools, possibly by allowing them to change status without consulting the parents. The Government accepted that there would be little prospect of any substantial increase in the number of GM schools before the next General Election, not least because taking all voluntary-aided schools out of LEA control would cost about 163 million pounds in the first year (see *TES*, 3 November 1995). Nevertheless, the Prime Minister and senior ministers had staked their credibility on reviving interest in the GM sector. They believed that the legislation could be used to embarrass the Opposition in the key months before the election. Despite the Labour Party's policy to end GM status, some senior Labour MPs sent their children to GM schools. The Conservatives were keen to exploit this contradiction. The rule they drew upon was one to promote the interest of their party by ensuring election victory.

The Government wanted to introduce both pieces of legislation before the next General Election. This meant the legislative process had to begin as soon as possible. However, there was strong opposition to both issues. The churches were particularly unhappy with their schools being singled out in order to increase the size of the GM sector. The Government was likely to face opposition from the Bishops in the House of Lords when introducing the GM bill. The Nursery Education Voucher Scheme was also unpopular among the actors concerned. Childcare interest groups, local authorities, the opposition parties, teachers, parents, and even some Conservative MPs and councillors had campaigned against it (see chapter 5). The DfEE[11] would face tremendous pressure if the Government wanted to get both bills onto the statute book by the summer of 1996, in order to be implemented in time before the next General Election. This would be all the more difficult since the Government had a working majority of only five in the House of Commons (*TES*, 3 November 1995).

The Government eventually brought the two issues into one bill — the Nursery Education and Grant-Maintained Schools Bill. Despite the apparent differences of the two issues, they had a common theme — to create a demand-driven market for education provision. This was to be achieved by abolishing the domination of LEAs and encouraging independent provision. Regarding pre-school education, the Bill set out arrangements for making grants, delegation of grant-making and related functions, and requirements for inspections. Most importantly, it gave the Secretary of State for Education and Employment the power to make grants with regard to pre-school education. This paved the way for public funding to be allocated to independent institutions. Regarding GM schools, the Bill gave them the power to borrow against their assets. The fast track for church schools was not proposed due to opposition from churches.

The Nursery Education and Grant-Maintained Schools Bill had its first reading in the House of Commons on 10 January 1996. The first reading was a formality. The motion that the Bill be given a first reading was carried without discussion. The Bill was then printed and made available to Members of the House for consideration before the second reading.

The second reading of the Bill was on 22 January 1996.[12] The second reading is the occasion for MPs to debate the principles of a bill. If a bill passes this stage of legislation, this means the House accepts it in principle. As was the case with the majority of legislation, the second reading of the current Bill was basically a battle between the Opposition and the Government.

Despite previous disagreement, government ministers united to press the Government's policy proposal through Parliament. They stressed the main theme of the Government's education policy, which was also the theme of the Bill, was to enhance parental choice and diversity of provision. Choice and diversity would contribute to raise quality. As the Secretary of State for Education and Employment argued (concerning pre-school education), through the provision of vouchers, 'parents will be in charge. They will choose the setting — state, independent or voluntary ...

(A)ll providers ... will be required to work towards the same educational outcomes; and ... will have to satisfy a common inspection regime.' (*Hansard*, 22 January 1996, Col. 24). The ideology behind this 'choice and diversity' argument was actually that of the right-wing — to create a market for educational provision. The right-wing ideology was the dominant ideology of the Conservative Party at that time. This theme of choice and diversity was appealing to the majority of Conservative MPs who supported the legislation.

For the Opposition, the voucher proposal was not a desirable way to expand under-fives provision. It would not provide choice and diversity as claimed by the Government. As the Education Spokesman of the Labour Party commented, the Government's proposal was 'offering people not a place, but a piece of paper promising that they can have a place in an area that does not have a place.' Ministers 'then call it a choice when they do not even have a place for them, let a lone a choice between providers. The slogan is simple — no place, no choice; no place, no nursery provision.' (Ibid., Col. 46). Apart from acting as the Opposition to the Government, the rule of the Labour Party was to ensure the expansion of pre-school education in a cost effective way. They rejected the Government's proposal which they thought would not achieve the purpose.

The attempt by the Opposition to lobby against the voucher proposal, however, was overshadowed by the accusation of contradictions in the Labour Party's education policy from Conservative MPs. The Labour Party had been against selection in education. It did not support GM status and wanted to abolish GM schools and grammar schools which practiced selection in their admission procedures. However, some leading members of the Labour Party took advantage of selection and sent their children to grammar schools. Such a contradiction was explored extensively and continually in the debate. Only a short time after the Secretary of State started her speech to introduce the Bill, when talking about the Government's policy principle of enhancing parental choice, she spoke of 'a principle so firmly supported by the hon. Member for Peckham' (Ibid., Col. 25). This Labour front-bench MP had sent her son to a grammar school fifteen miles away from where they lived. Her case was mentioned again and again by the Conservatives during the debate. They were keen to embarrass the Opposition in order to weaken their campaign against the Government's policy proposal.

Not all Conservative MPs, though, supported the Government. The Conservative MP for Buckingham had attacked the proposed legislation by asking for the amount of 'dead-weight money' in the voucher scheme — 'the millions of pounds that will be handed out to well-to-do parents who are already paying out of their private income for children to go to nursery school' (Ibid., Col. 25). The Conservative Member for Colne Valley, although speaking in support of vouchers, warned the Government that 'It is ... crucial that we do not ... overload the new scheme with unnecessary bureaucracy and regulation ...' (Ibid., Col. 70). The Conservative Member for Bristol North-West spoke against the Government concerning GM schools due to the situation in his constituency (Ibid., Col. 75-79). The strongest opposition to the vouchers came from the Conservative Member for Meriden (Ibid., Col. 93-94). He told the House that the area he represented had 'a scheme far beyond that proposed by the Government.' Parents 'are happy with the existing scheme, which is worth 1,800 pounds per pupil'. They 'do not want a national scheme'. He said, 'It is wrong to have a bureaucratic complex and centralized system that offers every child 1,100 pounds — a system that is going to be extremely difficult to organize.' He wanted ministers to 'provide an exemption for councils with good records'. He appreciated ministers' concerns that some councils needed to be forced into providing a better nursery system. However, he thought that if the Government were to give parents real choice, they should provide local authorities greater choice in the first instance. He presented a petition from 12,000 parents in his constituency expressing such a demand.

This handful of Conservative members and the Opposition members who did not support the Bill were not able to intervene in or make a change to the Government's policy proposal. They did not have the resources the Government had to depend on for the success of legislation. When the Bill was put to the vote after the debate, the Conservative MP for Bristol Northwest voted against the Government and the Conservative MP for Meriden abstained. The rule they drew upon was to uphold the interests of the society groups they represented. They did not support the Government's legislation because they thought that it was not in the best interests of their constituents. However, the Government had the organisational resources of a majority of MPs in the House of Commons. These resources were mustered by party whips who ensured government back-benchers supported the Government. On this occasion, the majority of Conservative MPs chose to go along with the dominant ideology of the Party and support the policy of the Government. The Bill won the second reading by a majority of 32 votes.

After successfully passing the second reading, the Bill proceeded to the committee stage. The Bill was examined in detail, clause by clause, in Standing Committee (F). Members were appointed to the Committee by all political parties. The proportion of members from major political parties mirrored their proportion of seats in the House of Commons. It is a convention that once in committee, party political divisions are not always clearly defined.   Government back-benchers are free to criticize the government. On this occasion, the party leadership, including government ministers, made use of their authority in appointing committee members and did not appoint any of the Conservative MPs who had originally criticized the Bill to the Committee (*Education*, 8 March 1996). Instead, the appointed Conservative members included ministers and right-wingers who were enthusiastic about a demand-led market for education.

For the Opposition, as the principle of the Bill had already been accepted by the House, all they could do was to propose amendments to improve the content of the Bill. The Standing Committee (F) met 15 times between 30 January and 5 March.   The Labour and Liberal Democrat members tabled more than 40 amendments.[13]   Regarding pre-school education, the Opposition sought to introduce measures to ensure the quality of provision, to make provision for capital expenditure, to restrict the power of the Secretary of State to make funding arrangements, and to prevent increased bureaucracy, inefficiency and fraud. They asked for a full evaluation of Phase One before any attempt was made to extend the voucher scheme nationwide.   Fundamentally, they did not agree that a voucher scheme would be the best way to increase pre-school education provision.   They proposed an alternative approach which would require LEAs to agree to a development plan with local providers. Conservative members disagreed with all of the Opposition's amendments. They were especially opposed to the development plan which was at odds with the Government's desire to create a market for pre-school education provision. Ministers had control over information concerning the more detailed arrangements of the Government's policy proposal which were not explained in full in the Bill.   They made use of this information, emphasized their own arrangements and dismissed the Opposition's amendments as not necessary. They were able to intervene in the decisions of the Opposition who withdrew many of their amendments before putting them to the vote. All those Opposition amendments which were put to vote were defeated. This was easily achieved because the Conservatives had a majority in Committee and all of them were supporters of the proposed legislation.

After the committee stage, the Bill underwent a report stage and a third reading on 19 March 1996. The Opposition continued to organize their effort to press for a better Bill. They once again tabled a considerable number of amendments.   These involved similar concerns to those proposed during the committee stage. Again, as in Committee, ministers used the information they had concerning the detailed arrangements of the policy initiative which were not explained in full in the Bill and argued that the Opposition's proposals were not necessary. They exercised power over the Opposition who withdrew many of their amendments. When Opposition amendments were put to the vote, they were all defeated by the majority of government MPs.

A major Opposition amendment would have allowed LEAs to 'opt-out' of the scheme where several conditions were met. These conditions included agreement by at least three-quarters of LEA members, wide consultation, the production of an alternative plan for the expansion of pre-school education in discussion with private and voluntary providers, and showing that not opting out would cause damage to the existing provision. This amendment was supported by the Conservative Member for Meriden who had pressed for LEAs with a high level of provision, just like Solihull in his constituency, to be allowed to opt-out of the scheme. Based on the rule of upholding the interests of the society groups he represented, he voted against the Government when the amendment was put to the vote. Apart from him other Conservative members voted for the Government. They defeated the Opposition's amendment by 276 to 238 votes.

Some of the issues raised by opposition amendments were reflected in the Government's own amendments. The government amendments were mainly of a technical nature and did not affect the rationale of the voucher proposal. Measures were introduced to ensure the quality of provision, to restrict the power of the Secretary of State in making funding arrangements for pre-school education. There was also an amendment to extend the power of LEAs to sell services related to Special Educational Needs (SEN) to GM schools, private or voluntary institutions. The Government made this concession after it had been strongly pressed by the Conservative Member for Mole Valley, a former Secretary of State for Education, who had been involved in fund-raising for the Royal London Society for the Blind. Ministers required legitimacy (as resources) granted by Parliament in order to carry out the policy initiative. They had to secure a certain degree of support in the House of Commons in exchange for such legitimacy. Therefore, they had to modify some of their policy preferences in response to the demands of the members of the House, especially those of the government members. However, ministers had autonomy over which of their preferences to modify and the extent of the modification. They had rejected this Conservative member's earlier suggestion of a differential voucher system which would recognize the extra costs involved in teaching SEN children. After the discussion on amendments, the Bill had its third reading. This was almost a formality. After some brief debate a vote was taken. On the government side the MP for Meriden abstained. The Bill with amended clauses passed its third reading by 272 to 238 votes.

The Bill then moved to the House of Lords for consideration. It passed through a similar legislative process as that of the House of Commons. The

House of Lords is the non-elected second chamber of Parliament. Peers are typically more independently minded than MPs and less fearful of the party whips. Despite ostensibly representing party interests, it is a convention for them to speak for themselves. On the occasions that the Government has faced little effective resistance in the House of Commons, the House of Lords has played a significant role in scrutinizing government activities. Surveys (Rush, 1990; Baggott, 1992; in Baggott 1995) have confirmed that the House of Lords is a favourite focal point for interest groups' lobbying, especially when their views are ignored by the government. On this occasion, interested organizations and persons who opposed the voucher proposal lobbied peers heavily. Many letters were sent to individual peers and briefing material by major interest groups was distributed in the House. As the Conservative peer Lord Tope told the House, 'It is unusual for your Lordships' House to receive quite so many letters from parents, teachers, heads and organizations who are concerned about the Bill' (*Official Report*, House of Lords, 20 May 1996, Col. 674). In the second reading, many Peers quoted extensively from these sources to demonstrate opposition to the voucher scheme. However, the minister for education argued that despite the Lords' concerns, virtually all of them had spoken of the benefits of expanding nursery education. The Bill would provide for just that. At the end, the Lords agreed to the principle of the Bill.

The detail of the Bill was then discussed in a Committee of the Whole House, followed by a report stage and a third reading. On all the three occasions, noble Lords carried out lengthy discussions on amendments to the proposed Bill. Many of the proposed amendments revealed similar concerns to those expressed in the House of Commons. With regard to the issue of pre-school education, the rule of the Lords was one to ensure the expansion of provision in a cost effective way. They did not think the proposed voucher scheme would achieve the purpose. However, almost all of the Lords' amendments were opposed by ministers. They said that the amendments would impose too many prescriptive measures or regulations on bodies which were to implement the policy, and thus were 'unnecessary'. The proposed amendments by the peers were either withdrawn or defeated, apart from those which came under government amendments and one opposition amendment. The government amendments were mainly of a technical nature, related particularly to SEN children, regulation specifications and admissions. The opposition amendment which went through was one to delay the nationwide implementation of the voucher scheme until an evaluation of Phase One had been laid before Parliament. This amendment was supported by a majority of peers and was carried by 92 to 58 votes. As it was unlikely that Phase One would be evaluated before the Autumn of 1997 — well after the last possible date for a General Election, this amendment would in effect delay the voucher scheme from being implemented nationwide until after the next General Election. The Labour Party had stated that if it came to power it would honour existing vouchers but would issue no more (*The Independent*, 19 June 1996). Therefore, under this amendment, if the Conservative Party were to lose the election, the voucher scheme would never come into existence nationally.

Opposition parties, local authority organizations, teachers unions and most childcare interest groups welcomed the amendment. However, government ministers insisted that it would overturn the Lord's amendment and the voucher scheme would go ahead nationwide in 1997. When the Bill returned to the House of Commons for consideration of the Lords' amendments on 17 July 1996, all government amendments were accepted. The main debate was on the opposition amendment. The Government argued that a delay of nationwide implementation until the result of an evaluation of Phase One was known would be unnecessary and damaging. Evaluation of Phase One was already being carried out. Delaying nationwide implementation would only deny four-year-olds the chance of having quality pre-school education. With a majority of government MPs in the House of Commons, this Lords' amendment was defeated by 275 to 251 votes (*Hansard*, 17 July 1996).

The Commons reason for rejecting the Lords' amendment was considered in the House of Lords on 22 July 1996. It is a long standing convention of the House of Lords that if a Bill originating in the House of Commons is examined and amended by the Lords, and that amendment is not agreed when the Bill returns to the Commons, that is the end of the matter. The Lords, being non-elected, did not have the same degree of legitimacy to make policy as the MPs. As the Labour peer Lord Morris of Castle Morris explained, 'We are the non-elected, revising and debating Chamber, and if our advice is rejected then the will of the elected body should prevail' (*Official Report*, House of Lords, 22 July 1996, Col. 1219). It is permissible for the Lords to table a further amendment, which if passed, would require the Commons to consider and vote again. However, this is an extreme action which would upset the convention. On this occasion, although a number of peers admitted 'sadness' and 'sorrow', the Lords agreed to follow convention and not insist on their previous amendment. The Nursery Education and Grant-Maintained Schools Bill received the Royal Assent on 24 July 1996.

To sum up, although there were some opposition voices in Parliament, the Government's proposal of pre-school education vouchers gained the legitimacy needed to go ahead. Opposition MPs, peers and the handful of Conservative MPs who disagreed with the Government were not able to intervene in or make changes to the Government's policy proposal. They did not have the resources that would enable them to do so. On the contrary, government ministers had some crucial resources in legislating. They had access to the information concerning the policy proposal which was not explained in the Bill. They had the organisational resources of a majority in the House of Commons. These resources were mustered by party whips who ensured government MPs supported the Government. As the party leadership, the leading members of the government had the authority in appointing members to Committee. In addition, as elected members in Parliament, MPs had a higher degree of legitimacy in policy making than the peers. With such centralized resources, government ministers were able to exercise power over other state actors in the democratic institution of Parliament. They were able to successfully press their policy proposal through Parliament despite opposition from many quarters. They were also able to intervene in some Parliamentary actors' actions and decisions, which led to the withdrawal of amendments by the Opposition. Although the central state actors had to modify some of their policy preferences in exchange for sufficient support, they had control over which preferences to modify and the extent of the modification. Therefore, the leading members of the government had a high degree of autonomy in the legislation stage. They enjoyed both type I* and type II* state autonomy. The significance of the democratic institution of Parliament in the policy process was to provide legitimacy for the Government to carry out their policy proposal very much according to their own will. The Parliament was of little significance in stopping the Government's policy proposal from going ahead. As an MP commented,

> The legislature here is not very powerful, certainly with the nursery voucher scheme. ... Power is very concentrated here on the Executive. Legislature too often is a rubber-stamp of the Executive, even in looking through legislation. (Interview A)

Conclusion

This chapter reviewed the policy stages of 'agenda setting', 'option selection' and 'legislation' of the Nursery Education Voucher Scheme. The Government made the decision to expand pre-school education through a universal voucher scheme. The policy initiative gained legitimacy to go-ahead after the necessary legislation had been passed by Parliament. Under the scheme the provision would be mostly part-time and for four-year-olds only. A provision in this form would have little effect on improving the employment prospects of women with young children. This was despite the fact that the discussion of a policy initiative to expand under-fives provision was originally driven by the demands in society for more childcare facilities in order to help women to take up employment. All the proposals that would favour women's employment opportunities were not adopted.

A combination of factors influenced the development of the voucher scheme. The social and political demand in society for more childcare facilities, and the need of the economy for mothers to go back to work in order to meet the projected labour shortage, led the Government to pay serious attention to the childcare issue. However, the leading members of the government, including the Prime Minister, ministers from the Treasury Office and other right-wing ministers, had a high degree of autonomy in deciding what was to be on the government's policy agenda and what should become the focus of policy action. They decided to provide pre-school education for four-year-olds, instead of a provision that would involve the element of care or would include children younger than four. The provision was to be made by public as well as independent institutions. Their decisions were made drawing upon the rules to control public spending and to enhance the traditional family and motherhood. Previous childcare policy, which had given separate consideration to care and education, and had been reluctant to develop the public sector, had effects on their decisions too. The leading members of the government were able to act autonomously in setting the policy agenda because they had the resources crucial for developing policy and expanding under-fives provision. The Prime Minister had the authority to oversee the work of the Government, including what was to be on the policy agenda. Ministers from the Treasury had control over public financial resources. The right-wing ministers had the organisational resources of party-political support, since the right-wing ideology was the dominant ideology of the Conservative Party at that time.

The leading members of the government also had a high degree of autonomy in choosing a universal voucher scheme, from other policy options, to make the provision. They preferred a universal voucher scheme drawing upon the rules to create markets for the provision of public services, to minimize public expenditure, to enhance the traditional family and motherhood, and to promote the interest of the party by ensuring electoral support and election victory. Using their resources, they ignored the opposition of society interest groups to the voucher option. They also intervened in the decisions of the DFE who originally did not favour a voucher scheme.

During the legislation stage, government ministers united to press the required Bill through Parliament, despite previous disagreement. They had some crucial resources in legislating which allowed them a high degree of autonomy in Parliament. They had access to information concerning the policy proposal which was not explained in full in the Bill and hence not available to the Opposition. They had the organisational resources of a majority in the House of Commons. They had the authority in appointing members to committees. They also had a higher degree of legitimacy in policy making than the non-elected peers in the House of Lords. Using their resources, they successfully pressed the legislation through Parliament despite opposition from many quarters.

The result of the autonomy of the leading members of the government in setting the policy agenda, in choosing the policy option and in legislation, was a policy initiative which embodied the reproduction of the rules of these most powerful actors. The implication of these rules for policy making, especially the ones of controlling public spending and enhancing the traditional family and motherhood, was to spend the least amount of money on developing childcare provision and to reject the kinds of provision which would aid mothers to go out to work. Policy made in this way only helped to sustain the gendered division of labour at home and at work. It continued to marginalize women's capacity to participate fully in the public domain of employment, and hence their rights as citizens.

Notes

1   Data quoted in Randall, 1996, p. 179.
2   More commonly known as the Rumbold Report, named after the chair of the Committee Mrs. Angela Rumbold CBE MP.
3   'Schools' here include maintained nursery, primary (nursery and reception classes) and special schools, non-maintained special schools and independent schools (*Hansard*, 9 June 1995).
4   For example, the National Campaign for Nursery Education (NCNE).
5   For both the CPS proposal and the Adam Smith proposal, also see *The Times*, 9 January 1995; *The Independent*, 9 January 1995.
6   *The Times*, 14, 16 March 1995; *The Independent*, 17, 23 March 1995; *TES*, 17, 24 March 1995; *The Sunday Telegraph*, 19 March 1995.
7   Not including individual schools and members of the public (*Hansard*, 7 February 1995). For a list of these as well as a list of the organizations and institutions the task force met or visited, see *Hansard*, 7 February 1995.
8   The ECEF is an umbrella group representing 35 organizations interested in early years education.
9   Also see *The Times*, 7 April 1995; *The Independent*, 7 April 1995.
10   See *The Sunday Telegraph*, 30 April 1995; *The Daily Mail*, 2 May 1995; *TES*, 5 May 1995.
11   Previously the DFE, now merged with the Department of Employment to become the DfEE.
12   According to procedure, there should be at least two weekends between the first and

the second readings for proper deliberation. For Parliament procedures mentioned in this session, refer to David Davis MP (1997), *A Guide to Parliament*.

13 House of Commons session 1995-96, no. 278, *Minutes of Proceedings on the Nursery Education and Grant-Maintained Schools Bill*, 30 January 1996 - 5 March 1996.

5 Policy Negotiation

This chapter continues the examination of the policy process behind the establishment of the Nursery Education Voucher Scheme. It is concerned with the stage of 'policy negotiation'. This policy stage covers the period between the announcement of the scheme by the Secretary of State for Education and Employment in the House of Commons on 6 July 1995, to its trial in Phase One piloting areas in April 1996. During this time, ministers and civil servants in the DfEE carried out negotiations with actors concerned over the more detailed arrangements of the voucher scheme. I argued in the last chapter that the central state actors — the Prime Minister, ministers from the Treasury Office and other right-wing ministers were the most powerful in deciding what was to be on the policy agenda and what was to become policy. However, once the decision for a voucher scheme was made, it was left to the government department responsible — the DfEE, to work out the details. There was some overlap between the stage of policy negotiation and legislation with the later part of the negotiation stage taking place simultaneously with the legislation stage, after the latter started in Parliament in January 1996.

The policy negotiation stage featured a high degree of participation by society actors and actors at the periphery of the state (i.e. local authorities and the Audit Commission). Interested organizations and persons expressed their opinion through writing to newspapers, sending out press releases, talking to the press, or writing to ministers and politicians. Childcare interest groups generally welcomed the new money for pre-school education, but questioned whether new places would be created as there were no capital funds specifically for this purpose. Educational interest groups were particularly concerned about the quality of the provision. Organizations such as the British Association for Early Childhood Education (BAECE) and the National Association of Head Teachers (NAHT) were disappointed that there would be no money for training staff and that there was no specification for the qualification of teachers.[1] Local authorities were unhappy about the fact that part of the current government funding for their under-fives services would be taken away to fund the voucher scheme. They would only get the money back if they could take in as many four-year-olds as they did at present. In addition, there was concern over the provision of children with SEN, and the element of competition the scheme might introduce.

From the many issues raised during this stage, I focus on four major events. The first relates to the demands of pre-schools to receive the full voucher rate, having originally been only eligible for half the full rate. The second event is the campaign by childminders to be included in the voucher scheme. The third event I examine is the consideration given by local authorities to joining Phase One — the pilot scheme. The last one is concerned with the Government's consultation on the quality assurance regime of the voucher scheme and the desirable outcomes for early years learning. Apart from these four major events, I also briefly look at several other incidents. These include some local and national campaigns against the voucher scheme; the worry expressed by Audit Commission, the Government's official watch-dog, that vouchers would destroy the co-operation between the public and the independent sectors; and the alternative plan proposed by the AMA which aimed to encourage co-operation between different sectors. The discussion examines how and to what extent various actors in society and at the periphery of the state were able to influence policy decision making in this stage of policy negotiation. Consequently, it shows whether it was the capitalists as argued by Marxism, interest groups as argued by pluralism, or state actors as argued by theorists of state autonomy, that were most influential in policy decision making in this policy stage.

Pre-schools — Demand for a Full-Rate Voucher

When the voucher proposal was first announced, the PLA gave it a cautious welcome. Despite all the short comings of the scheme, this was the first time in the 35 year history of the pre-school movement that member pre-schools were going to receive public funding as part of a national programme for the under-fives. However, a week after the announcement of the voucher scheme, during conversations with DfEE officials, PLA representatives were shocked to find out that pre-schools were only to be given a half-rate voucher. They would receive no more than 550 pounds a year for a child. This was half the value of a full rate voucher that other providers would get for each child attending the same number of sessions and under the same quality requirement. It was estimated that this arrangement would save the Treasury about 50 million pounds a year over the full rate. PLA representatives were very angry with such an arrangement. Their chief executive commented that this was 'totally unfair and totally insupportable'. It was 'in complete contradiction' to the principle of creating a free market pre-school education provision of the voucher scheme (*TES*, 14 July 1995).

The explanation offered by the DfEE was that officials had looked at pre-schools and found them inexpensive to run. Most of the settings were only costing parents about 2 pounds per session. As a result, pre-schools were given a half-rate voucher. However, the PLA argued that many pre-schools were already costing more than 550 pounds per child a year. Some of them needed additional funding to improve their facilities or to extend their provision for children currently attending less than five sessions a week. Representatives of the PLA made this issue public.[2] Their rule was one to uphold the interests of their members. They sent out press releases and received significant coverage in the national press. They encouraged members to write to their MPs about the issue. Many pre-schools threatened that they would not take part in the voucher scheme unless they were given more money. They received full support from the Liberal Democratic Party and the Labour Party.

In view of the PLA's strong response, the Under-Secretary of State for Education responsible for carrying out the voucher proposal wrote to the PLA. He assured them that if the level of the vouchers for pre-schools was deemed to be too low, the DfEE would look at it again. He held a meeting with the PLA in late July. Representatives of the PLA expressed in the strongest terms their concerns. These included,

- if pre-schools were required to meet the same educational outcomes as other providers, then they should be treated in the same way as far as funding was concerned;
- the cut-rate vouchers for pre-schools would not cover costs in all groups and would prevent the expansion in hours, places and training which the Government had encouraged;
- any distinction between the value of vouchers for pre-schools and those for other providers should have been made clear at the outset, before the PLA's original response was published (*Under Five Contact*, September 1995).

The Under-Secretary of State did not participate in the discussion in the earlier stages of the voucher scheme. He agreed that many pre-schools were providing quality education for four-year-olds no less, if not more, effectively than other forms of provision. There was no reason why they should receive half as much money as other providers meeting the same quality criteria. He promised to resolve the matter as soon as possible.

The most important reason for the Government's willingness to resolve the issue was the fact that pre-schools were seen as having the crucial organizational resources the Government had to depend on for the implementation of the voucher scheme. Over the years pre-schools had committed to providing quality pre-school education for the under-fives. They were, at that time, providing places for more than 200,000 four-year-olds. They were flexible in operation and cheap to run. The Government considered these factors as favourable conditions for the expansion of pre-school education. They saw pre-schools as having a vital role in providing extra places to cater for the 150,000 four-year-olds who had not yet got a pre-school education place (*Childcare News*, August 1995). The co-operation of pre-schools was important for the success of the voucher scheme.

With their crucial resources, pre-schools were able to influence the policy decision. They successfully intervened in and made a change to the Government's policy preference. Ministers eventually agreed to the demand of the PLA and member pre-schools. They announced the decision to offer pre-schools a full-rate voucher on 6 October 1995.

Childminders — Campaign for Inclusion

Childminding, which is one of the major forms of provision for the under-fives, was excluded from the voucher scheme. Vouchers could not be used for services provided by childminders. The NCMA and member childminders were very unhappy with such an arrangement. The NCMA made a vigorous response and published a press release on the day the scheme was announced. Their rule was one to uphold the interests of their members. They argued that the provision of nursery education vouchers was 'not the best use of the scarce resources available for pre-school provision'. The voucher scheme did 'not tackle the problem many parents face — the complete absence of choice in education and care'. By contrast, it had 'effectively denied parents the choice of using the new vouchers across the full range of market provision that exists for the under-fives'. It was widely recognized in the early years field that it was the quality of provision, whether centre or home based, that was important to young children. The voucher scheme 'ignored current research by acknowledging only group care was "educational"'. The NCMA was 'deeply concerned' that the voucher scheme might 'adversely affect the livelihood of nearly 150,000 self-employed childcare workers ..., without necessarily improving the quality of life for the children for whom they currently provide education and care' (NCMA, 6 July 1995).

At their AGM in September, NCMA members debated an emergency resolution regarding the voucher scheme. Four hundred members of the

NCMA representing 50,000 registered childminders in England and Wales endorsed the resolution (*Nursery World*, 5 October 1995). It called on the NCMA to launch a campaign to urge the Government to include childminders in the voucher scheme. They argued that registered childminders had already provided the educational outcomes that parents wanted. Childminders should be given the same opportunity to demonstrate their competence and be assessed against the same standards as other providers eligible for the scheme.

Government ministers disagreed with the childminders' arguments. They did not believe it would normally be possible to provide a structured programme of educational activities outside a group setting. They instead suggested that childminders should consider forming pre-schools with other childminders in their areas. This would enable them to develop a structured programme of activities in order to work towards the desirable learning outcomes required by the voucher scheme.

Childminders were disappointed by the Government's reply. In the run-up to Phase One, some childminders in the pilot areas applied to be assessed as voucher redeeming institutions. Not surprisingly their applications were turned down and they were told that they had no right of appeal. Meanwhile, the legislation required for the national implementation of the voucher scheme — the Nursery Education and Grant-Maintained Schools Bill, was going through Parliament. The NCMA considered this as their last chance to change the Government's decision.

The National Executive Committee of the NCMA agreed to step up the campaign. Through the NCMA's quarterly journal *Who Minds?*, the chief executive wrote to member childminders urging them to campaign at the local level. They should write to their local MPs to invite them to become involved in their campaign. They should encourage parents to write to their local MPs saying that when the voucher scheme was introduced nationwide, they would like to use the vouchers for their childminders. As the Government said the voucher scheme was about parental choice, the letter said, 'so let parents have some!' (*Who Minds?*, Summer 1996). Childminders were also encouraged to get the local media interested in their campaign. At the national level, a campaign leaflet, 'Briefing on Nursery Education and Grant-Maintained Schools Bill', was produced to express the position of the NCMA and member childminders on the issue. The leaflet was distributed to interested persons and organizations. The chief executive of the NCMA also wrote to politicians and other organizations to ask for their support. In total 43 MPs, 8 peers and 7 organizations replied, some were more supportive than others. Among those supporters, 3 Labour MPs, 7 Conservative MPs, the PLA and the

Parents at Work, wrote to the Under-Secretary of State responsible for carrying out the voucher proposal to campaign on the behalf of childminders.[3]

The NCMA had drafted a 'Framework Document' to show how, they believed, childminders could deliver the 'desirable outcomes' for early years learning. Representatives of the NCMA met ministers on 26 June 1996 to share this draft document with them. In addition, they argued strongly that in some parts of the country, due to a shortage of places, the voucher scheme could only work if childminders were included. After the meeting, the SCAA and Ofsted considered the 'Framework Document'. Ministers also looked into other material presented by the NCMA. In October, four months later, the NCMA received a reply from the Under-Secretary of State for Education. The letter explained the Government's education advisers' comment on the matter: 'although they agree that a small proportion of childminders could work towards the learning outcomes, they do not believe that childminders would be able to meet all the quality requirements of the voucher scheme' (quoted in *Who Minds?*, Winter 1996).

In another letter written to an MP lobbying for childminders, the Under-Secretary of State revealed another concern. Ministers worried that parents may 'register as childminders in order to keep their own children at home and claim the value of the voucher'. The letter said, 'although parents of compulsory age children are able to educate their children at home with the local authority's approval, they receive no public money to do so' (quoted in Ibid.). The NCMA argued that these sorts of objections arose only because the people involved did not have the first idea about how local authorities register and inspect childminders, and they had not bothered to find out (Ibid.). Nevertheless, ministers did not think childminding was a desirable form of provision for pre-school education to be included in the voucher scheme. This was reinforced by the fact that, historically, childminding was seen as an alternative form of provision to daycare services, but not to pre-school education (see chapter 3). So unlike the pre-schools, childminders did not have the organisational resources which the Government considered as crucial for the success of the voucher scheme. They were unable to successfully persuade the Government to include them in the scheme.

The Under-Secretary of State assured the NCMA that he would review the matter in 12-18 months time. He encouraged the NCMA to promote the 'Framework Document' to their members, as well as to consider other elements of the quality assurance regime of the voucher scheme. The NCMA published the document, 'Children's Learning, the NCMA Framework for Delivering Desirable Learning Outcomes' (the 'Framework

Document') in April 1997. It set out examples and descriptions of good childminding practice which would lead to the delivery of the 'desirable outcomes' for early years learning. The NCMA encouraged member childminders to work within this framework. However, before any result was seen, the voucher scheme was replaced by the Labour Government in May 1997.

The campaign of pre-schools and that of childminders form a clear case for comparison. Both the PLA and the NCMA received funding from government departments and had close contact with government officials. They both should be considered as 'insider' groups. However, the PLA and member pre-schools succeeded in their campaign for a full-rate voucher, whereas the NCMA and member childminders did not succeed in their demand to be included in the voucher scheme. Pre-schools were seen as having a vital role in providing pre-school education for four-year-olds, but childminders were not. The possession of crucial resources gave the PLA and member pre-schools the capacity to exercise power over the Government and brought a change to the latter's policy preference. On the contrary, the lack of resources that were crucial for the voucher scheme deprived the NCMA and member childminders of an ability to influence policy decision making.

Local Authorities — Volunteer for Trial

After announcing the voucher proposal, ministers and civil servants in the DfEE held discussions with local authorities to invite them to participate in the pilot scheme. Local authorities had the statutory duty to regulate under-fives provision in their local areas. The Government had to obtain their agreement for their areas to take part in the pilot scheme. The Secretary of State for Education and Employment expected that 12 local authorities would volunteer to participate in Phase One, with around 10 per cent of the 150,000 four-year-olds not at pre-school education at that time residing within these authorities' areas. The deadline for volunteering was 31 July 1995, less than four weeks after the official announcement of the voucher scheme.

However, the voucher scheme was unpopular among local authorities. In the first instance, they did not like the funding arrangements. Apart from the limited amount of new money made available, the scheme would be funded by money recouped from current government funding to local authorities for under-fives services — the Standard Spending Assessment (SSA) under-fives sub-block. Under the new funding arrangement, 1,100 pounds for each four-year-old currently in local authority provision would be deducted from the subsequent year's government funding for under-fives. Thus, a smaller intake the following year would result in a loss of 1,100 pounds for every child under the present number. Local authorities were worried that such an arrangement would endanger their existing provision, especially the provision for children younger than four. This was because the under-fives sub-block was to fund services for the under-fives, whereas the money recouped would be used for four-year-olds only. The new funding arrangements would also have the effect of punishing local authorities which had a high level of provision for four-year-olds, because more money would be taken away from their SSA to fund the voucher scheme. Figures compiled by the research division of the House of Commons library at the request of a Labour MP showed that seven local authorities would loose more than 10 million pounds by joining the voucher scheme. For Essex County Council whose under-fives grant was 28.85 million pounds in 1995, 16.33 million pounds would be clawed back under the scheme. From Hampshire, 16.23 million pounds would be clawed back, and from Kent, 16.21 million pounds (*TES*, 4 August 1995).

Other than funding arrangements, local authorities were also wary that too few of the other details of the scheme were known. The DfEE had failed to answer many questions and had even admitted to still having to work out details of the scheme. This admission did not instil local councils with confidence when they came to consider joining Phase One.[4] As a councillor commented,

> It (the voucher scheme) was launched as an act of panic by the Conservative Government who were very keen to sell it as fast as they could ... (W)e considered the proposals as they were at the time to be so ill defined ... It was all a bit last minute. It was very prescriptive but it lacked the detail ... (Interview B)

In addition to the general caution of local authorities, the Government was facing another problem. After the 1995 local council elections, only 5 local authorities were controlled by the Conservatives. The local council organizations were overwhelmingly controlled by Labour and the Liberal Democrats who had been strongly against the voucher scheme. The chair of the education committee of the AMA and that of the Association of County Councils wrote to the chairs of the education committees of all 117 metropolitan and county authorities in England and Wales to ask them to boycott the scheme. They said that they could offer 'no encouragement' to any council to volunteer to try out the vouchers (*The Daily Mirror*, 21 July 1995). Most of the local councils which were controlled by Labour or the Liberal Democrats expressed no interest in joining Phase One.

The opposition to the scheme was not just party political. Even some Conservative councillors were not keen on it. The Solihull County Council which was run by a Conservative-Independent coalition was an example. The chairman of their education committee and two officers were among those invited by the DfEE to discuss the possibility of joining Phase One. However, the education committee voted unanimously against participation. The chair of the committee, who was also the leader of the AMA Conservative group, commented that the voucher scheme would 'hijack' nurseries (*TES*, 28 July 1995). All four-year-olds in Solihull were already in local authority school reception classes and 73 per cent of three-year-olds were receiving publicly-funded pre-school education. As a comprehensive provider for the under-fives, Solihull would lose 2.9 million pounds of the 3.3 million pounds the Government currently allocated to the Council for under-fives services (the Council had topped this up to 6 million pounds). For the funding lost, money would have to be deducted either from other education budgets or from the early years budget itself. Although the Council would get back the money if it could take in the same number of four-year-olds as at present, the Council would not know how many, if any, parents would use their vouchers at the Council's schools. This was because parents could use vouchers in private and voluntary institutions as well as local authority ones. It was impossible for the Council to plan its budget in the face of such uncertainty (*TES*, 6 October 1995). For all the above reasons, the Council decided not to join Phase One. The rule of local councillors was to uphold the interests of their Council. They did not wish to participate in the pilot scheme since participation would not be favourable to such interests.

Nevertheless, local authorities which were controlled by the Conservatives were the majority among those few considering participation. By the deadline 31 July, two Conservative controlled local authorities had formally indicated interest in joining Phase One — Buckinghamshire and Wandsworth. Among the two, only the London Borough of Wandsworth offered a firm commitment to participate, Buckinghamshire's decision had yet to be confirmed. However, most of the three- and four-year-olds in Wandsworth already had pre-school places (*TES*, 28 July 1995). Trying out the scheme there would do little to prove whether vouchers were able to expand provision. It would only subsidize those who were currently paying for a place in a private institution.

Buckinghamshire was the only Conservative-controlled shire county. The Council saw joining Phase One as providing the opportunity to explore the expansion of under-fives education in their area. However, there was a number of outstanding questions which councillors considered would need to be answered before there was a commitment to enter Phase One.[5] These questions included how the voucher scheme would actually operate, its implications for existing provision and present funding arrangements, as well as potential inequalities of access to places given that there were not enough of them. Discussions were held between representatives of the Council and the DfEE to seek resolution of councillors' questions. Consultation was also carried out in the County with school governing bodies.

Due to the lack of response, the deadline for application for Phase One was postponed. In September, another Conservative-controlled authority, the London Borough of Westminster, announced their intention to join the pilot scheme (*TES*, 29 September 1995). They decided to try out the vouchers despite the fact that many of their councillors and officers had reservations. When joining Phase One the Borough would have to create 1,000 extra places in order to cater for all the four-year-olds. They planned that 700 of these would be in voluntary pre-schools and private schools, and another 300 would be provided by their own maintained schools. The new provision in the independent sector would cost 450,000 pounds a year. It would need another 100,000 pounds in capital costs, training and management. The Borough asked the DfEE to help to meet the capital costs, and further discussions were held. In addition to Westminster, the Conservative controlled London Borough of Kensington and Chelsea also were planning to join Phase One. Their representatives were having further discussions with the DfEE.

The only local council which was considering participation but was not controlled by the Conservatives was Norfolk County Council. The Conservatives lost power in Norfolk in 1993. Although it was then controlled by Labour and the Liberal Democrats, the fact that the county included the constituency of the Secretary of State for Education and Employment may have led to their increased interest in the voucher scheme. In addition, the Council saw some financial advantage in joining the pilot phase. The Council had a low rate of provision for the under-fives — only 34 per cent in January 1994 (*TES*, 20 October 1995). There were also few private nurseries in the County. The Council hoped to take the opportunity to expand their under-fives provision. They planned to open six more nurseries over the following year. They would then receive more vouchers from parents and hence more public money. However, councillors did have some reservations. By joining the pilot scheme, 7 million pounds would be clawed back from their current SSA under-fives sub-block. The Council carried out discussions with the DfEE about the precise amount they would have to contribute. Councillors argued that this money should be calculated fairly and should not be detrimental to the interests of the local authorities participating in Phase One. Also, the amount of contribution should not be subject to significant change in Phase Two. The Council asked for an 'escape clause' which would allow them to opt-out of Phase One and take back the money contributed should any insoluble problems be encountered (*TES*, 29 September 1995).

In Buckinghamshire, after a series of meetings and discussions, the education committee ruled out joining Phase One. Committee members did not think the questions raised by councillors had been resolved satisfactorily.[6] They were still unclear about how the system would actually operate, its impact on existing provision and on current funding arrangements. Committee members were particularly unhappy with the fact that the funding arrangement of the voucher scheme was unable to take into consideration the complexity and specificity of the current funding arrangements of the Council. The Council was currently providing part-time education for children in the term in which they reached the age of five — the rising-five term. Most children were admitted to nursery classes for the two terms preceding the 'rising-five term' on a part-time basis. The funding for this provision was made through the Local Management Scheme (LMS) formula. The rate for the rising-fives was 336 pounds per pupil in 1995/96 and 640 pounds per pupil in nursery classes. In addition, there were six nursery schools in the county catering for three- and four-year-olds. They were not part of the LMS but received funding through another pupil-based formula. The rate in this case was 821 pounds per pupil. The formula funding only accounted for part of each school's budget. The rest was made up of fixed allowances, premises allocations and other formula allowances. The funding arrangement of the voucher scheme, which would deduct from the subsequent year's government funding 1,100 pounds for each four-year-old in their provision, was unable to take into account the complexity of these existing funding arrangements.

Moreover, the DfEE proposed to count eligible pupil numbers for SSA deduction in Phase One authorities based on the number of four-year-olds in their maintained provision in 1994/95 academic year, and re-count the number in Phase Two based on those in provision in 1995/96. Committee members were unhappy about the fact that if the authority increased its provision in Phase One, it would suffer a greater deduction from its SSA in Phase Two. Furthermore, some committee members considered that the Council's surplus capacity for taking in pupils was approximately 7,800 places. Even if all these places were filled, a significant number of four-year-olds still would not have places and would have to use vouchers in facilities in the independent sector. It was estimated that a high percentage, about 40 per cent of vouchers (and hence voucher money) would have to go to the independent sector. In addition to the committee members' reservations, 75 per cent of local authority schools voted against joining

Phase One (AMA, June 1996). Consequently, in the education committee meeting at the end of November, the vote for joining Phase One was defeated by 18 to 17. Despite the Conservatives (including chairman and vice-chairman of the committee) pressing for the County to enter the pilot phase, Labour, Liberal Democrat and independent councillors, representatives of the Churches and one rebel Conservative, voted against it. The result of the vote reflected widespread unease about the voucher scheme in the County. The ruling Conservatives were accused for their act of 'blind political faith' (*TES*, 10 December 1995). The rule of other committee members was one to uphold the interests of their own County. Since joining Phase One would not be favourable to such interests, they did not support it.

Towards the end of 1995, the attempt of the Government to persuade local authorities to participate in Phase One was settled with four volunteers. Apart from Buckinghamshire, the other four authorities which had been considering joining agreed to participate. They were the London Borough of Kensington and Chelsea, the London Borough of Westminster, the London Borough of Wandsworth, and Norfolk County Council. All four authorities saw the possibility of influencing the scheme during its initial phase as the main reason for agreeing to participate. They had held many meetings with the DfEE since August 1995. A number of changes had been negotiated through the discussions.[7] A major concession allowed the voucher income to be made to local authorities instead of directly to their schools as it was originally planned. Local authorities would then distribute the money to their schools through the authorities' LMS system, as they did currently. Such discretion had let all authorities opt to pay grants to their schools in advance against the projected number of pupils. This was actually against the original intention of a market-led principle of the voucher scheme. However, no authorities would have agreed to participate in Phase One if this concession was not made. They considered that the burden on their schools, both administratively and financially, would have been too great otherwise.

Another concession made was on capital funding. As mentioned earlier, some councils had requested government help with the capital costs for the creation of new places. After negotiation, all four authorities were given the opportunity to apply for Supplementary Capital Approvals over two years. Capital allocations were also agreed with all four authorities. The DfEE stressed that this was only a transitional measure. It expected that the existing finance initiatives available for local authorities would play an increasing role in the provision of capital expenses in Phase Two. The third concession made gave all Phase One local authorities a guarantee that in the unlikely event of the voucher scheme not being able to go ahead, the authorities could have their SSA deduction restored. The fourth concession provided grants to the local authorities towards administration and publicity. These were estimated on a per head of population basis. The fifth concession accepted the provision of two sessions a week, rather than the suggested minimum of three, in response to a request from pre-schools in Norfolk. The final concession allowed voucher payments to be made on a half-termly rather than a termly basis as originally planned. Apart from this last change, the other concessions were only applicable to Phase One.[8] These arrangements brought the purpose and usefulness of a pilot scheme into question. Particularly with the extra financial help for capital expenditure and for the costs of administration and publicity, the pilot phase would not reveal the real feasibility of the voucher scheme, and the degree to which it could lead to expansion in provision.

Nevertheless, the Government had to make the above concessions in exchange for the participation of the four local authorities. Local authorities were regulators of under-fives services in their local areas. The Government had to depend on their authority to allow their areas to participate in Phase One. Local authorities were also providers in the public sector. They had the organizational resources the Government needed for the implementation of the voucher scheme. The rule of the local authorities was to secure their own interests against financial lost and against adverse effects on their current provision. They would not have joined Phase One if doing so were unfavourable to their interests. With their control over the crucial authoritative and organizational resources, they were able to intervene in the Government's decisions and requested a number of changes to the latter's policy preferences. However, even with the concessions made, only four (out of 108 in England) local authorities agreed to join the pilot phase. In total they contained only around 3 per cent of the four-year-olds not at pre-school education at that time (*The Independent*, 3 November 1995). This was far short of the Government's target of 10 per cent in 12 local authorities.

In view of the concessions made and the lack of participation in Phase One, it can be argued that the autonomy of the central state actors was challenged due to their dependence on the crucial resources of the local state actors for the implementation of the voucher scheme. However, their autonomy was only challenged partially. What most local authorities were against, but they were unable to intervene in, was the core components of the voucher scheme. These included the arrangements that 1,100 pounds would be re-couped from government funding for local authorities for every four-year-old currently in local authority provision in order to fund the voucher scheme; public funding would be distributed through vouchers to parents of every four-year-old to exchange for part-time pre-school education; and that vouchers could be used in the independent as well as the public sector. These core components were decided upon in the stages prior to this one of 'policy negotiation' — the stages of 'agenda setting' and 'option selection'. They were decided by the leading members of the government including the Prime Minister, ministers from the Treasury Office and other right-wing ministers (see chapter 4). After the decisions on the core components were made, the central state actors did not participate in the negotiation stage. They were simply too busy to do so and had to deal with other business of Government. The responsibility to carry out negotiation with the actors concerned was given to an Under-Secretary of State for Education in the DfEE. He was not involved in the discussions in earlier policy stages and was only given the job of making the voucher idea become a reality. Whatever concessions he made, he was not powerful enough to make any change to the core components of the voucher scheme. As he explained,

> From summer 94 to 95, I was not responsible for under-fives ... My involvement was to take a concept that had been determined by various committees and to turn it into a reality ... I had no say. I inherited the voucher decision. (Interview C)

Therefore, using the authority to allocate responsibilities to lower ranking ministers, the central state actors ensured that their policy preferences would not be challenged critically during resource exchange with other resourceful actors. Thus, any change made was not going to pose a threat to their values, beliefs, ideologies and interests upon which the core components of the voucher scheme were formulated. In this way, the leading members of the government in effect secured their autonomy in policy making.

Learning Outcomes and Quality Assurance

The Government emphasized that institutions redeeming vouchers had to provide education appropriate to a set of desirable learning targets, and they had to ensure the quality of their educational provision. While having discussions with local authorities about entering Phase One, the DfEE carried out consultation on learning targets and on the quality assurance regime. The DfEE and the DoH jointly issued the draft document 'Quality Assurance Regime for Institutions which Redeem Vouchers for Pre-School Education' in September 1995. The SCAA issued the document 'Pre-School Education Consultation — Desirable Outcomes for Children's Learning and Guidance for Providers' a week later. Responses were requested from interested organizations and persons.

The document 'Quality Assurance Regime' outlined issues which would need to be addressed by a regime aimed at ensuring the quality of pre-school education. These included adult-child ratios in pre-school classes, premises and equipment, SEN, inspection, public information for parents and training for early years workers. The deadline for consultation was 13 October 1995. The document 'Desirable Outcomes for Children's Learning' set out targets which an average child should be expected to achieve when entering compulsory schooling at the age of five. These targets covered six areas of personal and social development, language and literacy, mathematics, knowledge and understanding of the world, physical development, and creativity. All public, voluntary or private providers who wanted to participate in the voucher scheme would have to provide education which would lead children towards these desirable learning outcomes. The deadline for consultation for this document was 12 October 1995. The government departments responsible would then submit final versions of both documents to the Secretary of State for Education and Employment for approval and prepare them for publication for public use later on.

With respect to the quality assurance regime, interest organizations were, in the main, dissatisfied with the inspection arrangements, the difference in the requirements of adult-child ratio for different providers, and the provision for SEN children.[9]

In the case of inspection arrangements, it was widely recognized that the current dual system should be removed and that there should be a unified system of inspection for voucher redeeming institutions. The current dual system involved Ofsted carrying out inspections of maintained nursery schools and classes, whereas local authority social services departments carried out inspections of private and voluntary providers registered under the Children Act 1989. However, under the Government's proposal, in addition to the dual system, Ofsted would carry out a supplementary inspection on the educational aspect of the provision in private and voluntary institutions participating in the voucher scheme. Interest organizations considered such an arrangement as inappropriate since it created a third layer of inspection. It increased the burden on independent providers who would be inspected twice.

Regarding the adult-child ratio, private and voluntary institutions registered under the Children Act 1989 were required to have a ratio of 1:8. A ratio of 1:10 or 1:13 (depending on whether the headteacher did teaching or not) was permitted for premises registered as private nursery schools. For LEA-maintained nursery classes in schools, the guidance of the Children Act recommended a ratio of 1:13. This was not a regulation as nursery classes came under school regulations which did not specify an adult-child ratio. For the same reason, there was no specification of the adult-child ratio in reception classes in schools (AMA, June 1996). Interest organizations considered that such a difference in adult-child ratio requirement was inappropriate. They wanted a ratio of 1:8 in all settings regardless of the nature of the qualifications of the staff. This suggestion was opposed by local authorities. Their rule was one to protect their own interests. They argued that their pre-school classes were taught by qualified teachers and therefore should enjoy the requirement of a lower adult-child ratio.

Regarding the provision for SEN children, childcare and education interest groups generally supported the Government's proposal that voucher redeeming institutions should comply with the Code of Practice on the Identification and Assessment of Special Needs. However, they argued that additional measures including extra financial resources should be introduced, because teaching SEN children would require special facilities and skills. Also, LEAs should have a vital role in providing suitable training and support for SEN provision.

The responses to the 'desirable outcomes' were less critical. Early years workers were relieved that the learning outcomes set out by the SCAA were not overly prescriptive and largely based on good practice (*TES*, 15 September 1995). There were though concerns that in order to achieve these learning targets, high quality staff and premises, skills and equipment would be required. However, the Government was not prepared to provide extra financial help. There was also criticism that the learning targets represented too limited a view of children, and consideration of equal opportunities and cultural differences was limited. By the end of the consultation exercise, the SCAA received about 4,000 questionnaire responses and 200 detailed recommendations. It also received responses from a series of regional conferences. There was general support for the 'desirable outcomes' especially in the areas of creativity and imagination, although there was less support for the language and literacy guidelines. A common worry was how different early years workers with different qualifications were going to interpret these learning targets (*Nursery World*, 7 December 1995).

After the consultation, the Government published both documents on 9 January 1996. The DfEE document, *Nursery Education: The Next Steps*, outlined details of how vouchers were intended to work, quality assurance and inspection arrangements. The DfEE and SCAA document, *Nursery Education: Desirable Outcomes for Children's Learning on Entering Compulsory Education*, stated targets of learning children were expected to achieve when they entered compulsory education. Some changes were made to the 'desirable outcomes' to take account of criticisms. 'Personal and social development' included a clause to 'show respect for people of other cultures and beliefs', and children would be expected to 'respond to' rather than to 'take part where appropriate' in religious and cultural events (*Education*, 12 January 1996). References to the use of tape-recorders and computers had been removed in a response to requests from pre-schools which did not have sufficient facilities. It also included more emphasis on play, due to fears from early years educationalists that the learning targets would be used by untrained helpers to drill children (*The Guardian*, 10 January 1996). There was, though, continual criticism from interest organizations that the 'desirable outcomes' were 'narrow and lacking in depth'. It could lead to misguided efforts to introduce too formal an approach to education too early. It would be meaningless or ambiguous in the hands of untrained early years workers, but the Government had no plans to provide extra financial help to improve training (*TES*, 12 January 1996).

'The Next Steps' document had taken up few of the criticisms. With regard to the provision for SEN children, some minor changes were made concerning the role of the LEAs. However, no extra financial resources were made available despite the demand of interest organizations. Interest organizations continued to believe that vulnerable children would suffer further disadvantages under the voucher scheme (*Community Care*, 22-28 February 1996).

The Government maintained the original proposal on inspection arrangements despite strong criticism. The existing inspection of nursery classes and reception classes in schools by Ofsted and inspection of private and voluntary premises registered under the Children Act by local authorities would continue. In addition to these, Ofsted would inspect the educational aspect of the provision by private and voluntary institutions. These institutions would have to show they were working towards the 'desirable outcomes' for early years learning. Those who failed an inspection would lose their validation and might have to close. Ofsted was already overloaded by its existing task of inspecting primary schools in a four year cycle. It would need to recruit 300 more inspectors in Phase One and 4,000 more in Phase Two for day-long visits to pre-school education settings. Some private or voluntary institutions which were included for the first time in the regulation framework by Ofsted would be able to operate for nearly a year before being inspected. There was criticism that this latter arrangement could hardly guarantee the quality of provision (*The Independent*, 10 January 1996).

The only change in staffing arrangements was that nursery schools and nursery classes in primary schools would be required to have a staff-children ratio of 1:10 and 1:13 respectively, and half of the staff would have to be qualified teachers as at present. However, these tightened staffing arrangements would not be applied to reception classes. They continued to have no requirement on staff-children ratio, although all staff had to be qualified teachers. The voluntary sector, which was required to have a staff-children ratio of 1:8, was particularly disappointed by such an arrangement (*TES*, 12 January 1996; *Education*, 12 January 1996).

Summing up, opportunities were created for interest organizations and persons to express their views through the official consultation exercises on the 'desirable outcomes' for early years learning and the quality assurance regime. However, little critical change was made as a result of the consultation. The criticisms and demands of interest organizations were taken up very selectively. Little response was made to the strongest criticisms on adult-child ratio, inspection arrangements, extra financial help for the provision for SEN children and for the training of staff. Interest groups were ineffective in their attempt to intervene in and make changes to the Government's policy preferences. This was because they did not have the resources that were crucial for the success of the voucher scheme upon which the Government would have to depend. They could only express their opinion but had little real influence over policy decision making. The government departments responsible, authorized by the leading members of the government, were ultimately responsible for whether, and what aspects of, the original proposal were to be changed, and the extent to which they were changed. They had autonomy in policy decision making. Their autonomy was equivalent to Type I* state autonomy — their preferences on the 'desirable outcomes' for early years learning and the quality assurance regime were different from the preferences of society actors, they acted on their own preferences.

Participation of Other Interested Actors

Other than the four major events discussed, there were several other incidents of involvement by interested actors. Some local campaign groups were formed by parents or teachers from local authority schools to protest against the voucher scheme. The National Campaign for Nursery Education (NCNE) organized a Parliamentary lobby. The Campaign Against Vouchers in Education (CAVE) organized a national demonstration. The Audit Commission warned in its report that the voucher scheme could destroy the co-operation between the public and the independent sectors. The AMA proposed an alternative scheme which aimed to encourage the co-operation between different sectors. However, all the criticisms and recommendations had no effect on the Government's policy proposal. The interest organizations concerned did not have the resources that the Government would need for the success of the voucher scheme. They were unable to intervene in the Government's decisions.

Local authorities' reservation about the voucher scheme was supported by their schools. Some teachers and parents formed local campaign groups and organized lobbying against the voucher scheme. In Buckinghamshire, an effective anti-vouchers campaign was organized by parents and teachers form the council-run Henry Allen Nursery School (*TES*, 10 December 1995). As a nursery which specialized in teaching SEN children, campaigners worried that the nursery would not be able to provide this service anymore. Making provision for SEN children would cost much more than 1,100 pounds a year. However, there would not be extra funding other than the voucher money. Campaigners thought it was unfair that as a local authority maintained nursery, they could not take top up money from parents, in contrast to private institutions. The rule of the campaigners was to protect the interests of children and their schools. They lobbied against the voucher scheme as it would be unfavourable to such interests. With the general opposition in the county, the Conservative controlled local authority in Buckinghamshire decided not to join in Phase One (see previous discussion).

Another well-publicized local protest against the vouchers was based in Solihull. Head-teachers of the 72 LEA-maintained primary schools launched the campaign against the voucher scheme in October 1995 (*TES*, 6 October 1995). They called themselves the Solihull Primary Partnership of LEA Schools. They were unhappy with the fact that the money clawed back from their current funding would be given to the voucher agency, which would distribute the money through vouchers to parents to exchange for pre-school education at either local authority or independent institutions. They had reservations about the quality of provision by private companies. They thought it would be difficult to ensure the staff of private institutions had the correct training, knowledge and understanding necessary for early years learning. They campaigned for Solihull to opt out of the voucher scheme. Their rule was to protect the interests of their schools. They protested against the voucher scheme as it would be unfavourable to such interests. They rallied the support of parents and governors. They also gained support from their MP. This Conservative MP for Meriden had urged the Government to make the voucher scheme discretionary to allow LEAs with a high level of provision to opt out. He voted against the Government on a relevant Opposition amendment and abstained in the vote for the Nursery Education and Grant-Maintained Schools Bill (see chapter 4).

The view that pre-school education should be provided by LEA-maintained schools instead of independent institutions was echoed by the NCNE. The NCNE is a voluntary campaigning group founded in 1965 to promote the provision of quality nursery education in state-funded nursery schools and classes.[10] They considered the vouchers, which could be used to exchange for pre-school education in private and voluntary settings, a serious threat to the development of high quality nursery education. The NCNE organized a national campaign and lobbied Parliament on 25 October 1995 (*The Independent*, 26 October 1995). A few hundred people from all over the country gathered at the House of Commons. Among them were parents, children, nursery and primary school staff and governors, local authority councillors including a group of Conservative councillors. Speakers from all political parties addressed the rally. Some protesters had the opportunity to discuss the issue with ministers and representatives of other political parties in a meeting held in the House of Commons. After the meeting, the chair of the NCNE commented that it was apparent that the Government had no answer to the queries and criticisms they raised (*Nursery World*, October 1995).

Another national demonstration against the voucher scheme was organized by the CAVE and held on 16 March 1996.[11] CAVE was an anti-voucher group founded by parents and early years workers in Kensington and Chelsea and Westminster. It was set up after a National Union of Teachers (NUT) conference on nursery education and received funding from the NUT and Unison, the public employees' union. It had support from other national campaign organizations such as the NCNE, and local campaign groups which had appeared across the country like Kirklees Campaign Against Vouchers, Hounslow Early Years Campaign, Barnet Parents Against Vouchers, Solihull Parents Against Vouchers, etc. The demonstration started at Battersea Park in south London. The demonstrators marched through the three London local authorities which were taking part in Phase One, to the Central Hall in Westminster where a rally was held. Speakers from various campaign groups, unions and local authorities all spoke against the voucher scheme. After the rally, a delegation went to No. 10 Downing Street where campaigners presented the Prime Minister with a petition containing 50,000 signatures.

None of the local or national campaigns, however, were able to influence the Government's decisions and make a change to the proposal of a voucher scheme. CAVE and local campaign groups were issue-oriented and *ad hoc*. The NCNE was not consulted often by the government and should be considered as an 'outsider' group. None of them had the resources that the Government would need for the implementation of the voucher scheme. Consequently, they were unable to influence policy decision making.

The Audit Commission, the Government's official watch-dog, also expressed concern over the voucher scheme in its report, 'Counting to Five',[12] published on 26 January 1996. The report revealed that publicly-funded nursery education was very uneven across the country. The percentage of four-year-olds with a place in LEA-maintained nursery schools or primary schools varied from 26 per cent in Hereford and Worcester to 95 per cent in Knowsley and Merseyside. It was apparent that many LEAs would not be able to provide pre-school education for every four-year-old in their areas in the immediate future. In order for every voucher-bearing four-year-old to have a pre-school education place, LEAs would need help from independent providers. However, the co-operation between private, voluntary and public sectors could collapse under the voucher scheme. 'Some (maintained) schools may feel pressure to spend more in their nursery classes to compete with private nurseries. Others may feel compelled to spend more on their reception classes, to secure the enrollment of pupils ...'. 'Because support for the private and voluntary sectors is non-statutory, it could be vulnerable to cuts. It is possible that some local authorities will react defensively and concentrate attention on their own schools ... that private and voluntary providers will lose some of their interest in co-operation with local authorities.' The report warned 'if parents' choices become more volatile or competition more intense, some authorities may be exposed to greater financial uncertainty'. The rule of the Audit Commission was to ensure the proper use of public financial resources. It called for co-operation between all sectors for the success of the voucher scheme. It urged local authorities to take a leading role. They could supply premises or revenue support to independent providers, or use existing private and voluntary provision to ensure a wide range of services. It argued that if all sectors could co-operate and avoid crude competition, local authorities might be able to reduce the financial risk created by the voucher scheme (Audit Commission, 1996).

The prediction by the Audit Commission as to the impact of the voucher scheme was echoed by some interest organizations. A coalition of organizations comprising Barnardo's, the Children's Society, the National Early Years Network (NEYN), the National Council of Voluntary Child Care Organizations, Save the Children and the AMA, also thought that the voucher scheme would destroy the co-operation between the public sector and the independent sector (*Community Care*, 22-28 February 1996). They further argued that by introducing an element of competition, the scheme contravened the collaborative spirit of the Children Act 1989. The Act had given local authorities the functions of regulating provision offered by the private and voluntary sectors, and co-ordinating provision made by different agencies (see chapter 3). Up until that time local authorities had supported voluntary and private providers through grants, provision of authority premises at low rents, and payment of some children's fees. The NEYN, who supported such co-operation, was at that time servicing a network of 300 early years forums made up of statutory and voluntary agencies. Their chief executive pointed out there had been enormous benefits from these forums by sharing initiatives and information. Local authorities' support for the private sector had been incredibly important and local authorities had benefited from the services of community-based independent providers. By introducing an element of competition, the voucher scheme would put these collaborations under strain.

Again, the Audit Commission and the interest organizations did not have the resources that the Government would need for the implementation of the voucher scheme. They were unable to intervene in the Government's decisions. Despite their warnings, the Government took no preventive measures.

In view of the importance of co-operation between the public sector and the independent sector, and the prediction that the Government's proposed voucher scheme would destroy such co-operation, the AMA put forward an alternative proposal which aimed to encourage co-operation.[13] Under the AMA's proposal, LEAs and the private and voluntary sectors would make joint bids for funding to the DfEE based on a development plan for local services. The Government could use the forthcoming legislation on nursery education to place a duty on LEAs to work with private and voluntary providers to establish such development plans. The funding would come from the 165 million pounds designated for vouchers and the 20 million pounds allocated to administration and inspection under the voucher scheme. The money would be distributed through LEAs according to priorities set out in the development plans. This funding arrangement would not include the 548 million pounds which would be re-couped from local authorities' current under-fives funding under the Government's proposal. The AMA argued that the Government's proposal would penalize those LEAs with high levels of provision and would do little to create new places. However, under the AMA's proposal, high providers would have nothing to lose and low providers would have much to gain. The latter would be able to establish new places using all the new money available without it being diverted into administration.

The AMA's alternative plan was welcomed by many interested actors and the DfEE studied it closely. However, in the event the AMA's proposal was not adopted by the Government. The AMA had no resources that the Government would need for the implementation of the voucher scheme. Its suggestion had no effect on the Government's policy proposal.[14]

This part of the discussion looked at some other incidents in the stage of 'policy negotiation', other than the four major events discussed earlier. The activities of local campaign groups reinforced local authorities' opposition to the voucher scheme, yet they had no effect on the policy proposal of the Government. The Parliamentary lobby organized by the NCNE and the national demonstration organized by the CAVE also had no effect on the voucher proposal. The warning by the Audit Commission and other interest organizations that the voucher scheme would destroy the co-operation between the independent sector and the public sector, did not lead to the introduction of any preventive measures by the Government. In addition, the alternative proposal suggested by the AMA, which sought to encourage the co-operation between the public and the independent sectors, was not adopted by the Government. All these interested actors had no resources that the Government would need for the successful implementation of its policy proposal. They were unable to intervene in the Government's decisions and had no influence on policy making. The Government (ministers) had a high degree of autonomy in policy decision making with respect to these interested actors. Their autonomy was equivalent to Type I* state autonomy.

Conclusion

This chapter studied the policy stage of 'policy negotiation' of the voucher scheme. After the announcement of the scheme, discussions and negotiations were carried out between the DfEE and actors concerned. Four major events occurred during this stage. Pre-schools which were originally given a half-rate voucher successfully demanded a full-rate one. Childminders who were excluded from the voucher scheme did not succeed in their campaign for inclusion. Only four local authorities agreed to join Phase One to try out the vouchers. They successfully demanded a number of concessions from the Government in exchange for participation. Little change was made to the quality assurance regime and the 'desirable outcomes' for early years learning. This was despite some strong criticism from interest organizations. Apart from these four major events, there were other incidents. These included local and national campaigns against the voucher scheme, the warning by the Audit Commission and some interest organizations that vouchers would destroy the co-operation between the independent sector and the public sector, and the AMA's proposal of an alternative plan purported to encourage such co-operation. However, all these efforts had no effect on the Government's policy proposal.

In this policy stage we saw a high degree of participation by actors in society and at the periphery of the state, although there was no obvious presence of economic interest groups or capitalists. Interested actors sought to influence policy decisions by expressing their views through official consultation exercises, campaigns and lobbying activities, publication of discussion documents and press releases, writing or talking to ministers and other politicians, etc. Insiders such as the PLA, the NCMA and local authorities had more opportunities to negotiate directly with the Government. However, only pre-schools and the local authorities which were joining Phase One succeeded in their efforts to change some of the Government's policy preferences. They were able to do so because they had the crucial resources (organizational resources of the pre-schools, organizational and authoritative resources of the local authorities) on which the Government had to depend for the implementation of the voucher scheme. Other interest organizations were unable to intervene in the Government's policy decisions, since they did not have the resources that would allow them to do so.

Even groups which had the crucial resources were unable to make any change to the core components of the voucher scheme. These core components were decided upon by the leading members of the government drawing upon their own rules in the policy stages prior to this one of 'policy negotiation'. After making the respective decisions, they had little involvement in the negotiation with actors concerned. The responsibility was given to a lower ranking minister who did not participate in the discussions in the earlier stages. Whatever concessions he made he was not powerful enough to change the core components of the voucher scheme. Therefore, using their authority to allocate responsibilities to lower ranking ministers, the central state actors secured the influence of their values, beliefs, ideologies and interests on the form of the new policy initiative. In this way, they in effect ensured their autonomy in policy making. The 'gendered' aspect of the policy, that it largely assumed a traditional role for women, was unable to be challenged.

Notes

1   Reference is made to the respective letters to the Secretary of State for Education and Employment by the BAECE dated 12 July 1995 and by the NAHT dated 3 August 1995.
2   For the pre-schools' campaign for a full-rate voucher, also see *TES*, 14 July 1995, 11 August 1995; *Under Five Contact*, September 1995; *The Independent*, 7 October 1995; *Pre-school Learning Alliance Annual Review*, 1995.
3   According to internal documents provided by the NCMA.

4   For the general worries of local authorities also see *TES*, 28 July 1995; *The Independent*, 31 July 1995.
5   Reference is made to the minutes of council meetings and to material from an interview with a councillor.
6   For the concerns of the members of the education committee of Buckinghamshire County Council, reference is made to the minutes of meetings and briefing papers of the committee.
7   For the changes made also see AMA, June 1996; *The Independent*, 19 September 1996, and *Nursery World*, 4 July 1996.
8   The first concession, that voucher income would be made to local authorities instead of to their schools, was later extended to Phase Two.
9   For recommendations of interest organizations, also see NCB, Early Childhood Unit (1995), 'Quality Assurance Regime for Institutions which Redeem Vouchers for Pre-School Education', and *Co-ordinate*, November 1995, 'Assuring Quality with Vouchers'.
10 Based on information provided by the NCNE.
11 CAVE, demonstration leaflet; CAVE 'Planning Meeting for National Action 18.5.96: Minutes'; *Term Time*, April 1996; *TES*, 15 March 1996.
12 For the Audit Commission report, also see *TES*, 26 January 1996; *The Independent*, 26 January 1996; *TES*, 2 February 1996.
13 For the AMA's alternative proposal, also see *TES*, 3 November 1995; *Education*, 8 November 1995; and *Nursery World*, 4 January 1996.
14 An Opposition amendment to the Nursery Education and Grant-Maintained Schools Bill based on the AMA's proposal was proposed in Parliament, but was defeated (see chapter 4). The AMA's proposal was later enacted by the Labour Government after the Labour Party gained office at the 1997 General Election. This will be discussed in the next chapter.

6 Implementation and Replacement

This chapter continues the theme of the previous two chapters in examining the policy process of the Nursery Education Voucher Scheme. The last two chapters discussed the policy stages of 'agenda setting', 'option selection', 'legislation' and 'policy negotiation'. This chapter focuses on the final two stages of 'implementation' and 'replacement'. It was revealed in chapter 5 that no change was able to be made to the core components of the voucher scheme during the negotiation with actors concerned. After the negotiation stage, the voucher scheme with its core components was piloted in the four Phase One local authorities from April 1996. At that time the legislation necessary for Phase Two nationwide implementation was still going through Parliament. The required Bill received Royal Assent in July 1996. Phase Two started immediately after Phase One, in April 1997. This phase of nationwide implementation only lasted for one school term. The voucher scheme was replaced by the Labour Government after their election victory in the May 1997 General Election.

Within its 'necessary' components, the voucher scheme included a complicated mechanism of nine procedures. The first part of the chapter looks at the running of these procedures, the problems raised and the participation of the actors concerned. This part of the discussion also examines the effect of implementation (in this case, mainly in the Phase One pilot scheme) on policy decision making and thus on the form of the policy initiative. The second part of the chapter analyses the extent to which implementation achieved the designated aims of the voucher scheme and argues that these aims were not successfully fulfilled. The last part of the chapter is concerned with the replacement of the voucher scheme. The transference of resources and hence power from the Conservative Party to the Labour Party after the General Election gave the latter the autonomy to bring this political drama to an end.

Implementing the Vouchers: Process and Actors

After the policy negotiation stage, the voucher scheme was tried in the four Phase One local authorities. Public funding was distributed through vouchers which could be used by parents to exchange for part-time pre-school education for their four-year-olds in validated institutions. A complicated mechanism of nine procedures was derived for the purpose. First of all, the DfEE sent invitations to providers to ask them to take part in the scheme. Secondly, providers completed the application forms and returned them to the DfEE. Thirdly, the DfEE gave an initial validation to eligible providers. Fourthly, application forms were sent from the Child Benefit Centre (CBC) to eligible parents.[1] Then, parents filled in the forms and returned them to the Nursery Voucher Centre (NVC).[2] In the sixth procedure, the NVC checked the information of the children and sent vouchers to parents. In the seventh one, parents handed vouchers to providers. In the eighth one, providers collected vouchers and returned them to the NVC for redemption. Finally, the NVC reimbursed voucher money to providers. In the following, I will briefly explain the running of these nine procedures. I will also discuss the problems raised and the participation of the actors concerned.

The DfEE sent out invitation and information packs to providers in the four Phase One local authority areas from the end of 1995. It was not compulsory for providers in Phase One areas to join the voucher scheme. Providers who wished to take part were asked to fill in a self-assessment schedule (see AMA, June 1996, p. 9). To be eligible they had to agree to, 1) publish information for parents, including staff qualifications, premises and equipment; 2) work towards the 'desirable outcomes' for early years learning as recommended by the SCAA; and 3) be inspected regularly by Ofsted on their education provision; and 4) have regard to the Code of Practice on SEN. Upon submission of their application and the self-assessment schedule, establishments were granted initial validation without any formal inspection. Full validation would be given after a satisfactory inspection by Ofsted. This would be carried out within a year of the scheme coming into operation.

The application process for eligible parents started in January 1996. The first round of 14,000 forms were issued from the CBC (see Ibid., p. 17). A further 2,000 copies were issued from inquiries made to the NVC. Parents completed the application forms and returned them to the NVC. After checking the information of the child, vouchers were sent to parents. Vouchers were in the form of sheets of A4 with five separable parts. Each part could be used to exchange for one session (2.5 hours) of pre-school education in each week of a school term. Vouchers would be issued termly and the first round was for the coming summer term. Sent together with the vouchers was a booklet explaining how to use the vouchers and a list of providers. The latter contained up to 42 initially validated establishments within an 8 mile radius of the parents' address.

At the beginning of the summer term, parents handed in vouchers to providers. After providers collected the vouchers, they sent them on to redeem voucher money. An LEA-maintained setting either sent vouchers to the LEA which then returned them to the NVC, or sent them directly to the NVC, a matter for each LEA to decide. The NVC confirmed receipt to the DfEE which then reimbursed the LEA. In the case of GM schools, vouchers were returned directly to the NVC and the DfEE reimbursed the Funding Agency for Schools. In the case of non-maintained settings, providers returned the vouchers to the NVC and the DfEE reimbursed them directly.

Such a complicated voucher mechanism had caused confusion among parents and put an extra burden on them. Many parents whose children were in LEA-maintained settings found it hard to understand the purpose of the vouchers. As their children already had free pre-school education, many of them did not know why they needed vouchers. Some parents threw away the voucher application form. Some did not take good care of the form and lost it (e.g. eaten by dogs, see *TES*, 9 February 1996). Some other parents wanted to use the vouchers for other things such as school uniforms (also see Ibid.).

Not all parents had voucher application forms sent to them automatically. Those parents whose children were not on the CBC register, or those who had moved house, did not initially receive the application forms. They had to request the forms through the NVC telephone help-line. In the case of the information of the child on the application form being incorrect, parents also had to seek help through the telephone help-line. Although majority of the parents who had used the help-line found staff there were helpful (Unison, September 1996), there were parents who experienced difficulties. There was one case where the information of the child was wrongly printed again and again. The parents encountered considerable trouble and had to produce proof of identity for the child (*Nursery World*, 4 April 1996). With the complexity involved, it was particularly difficult for parents whose first language was not English to understand the scheme and to obtain vouchers. There were a considerable number of such parents in the London Boroughs in Phase One. In addition, most parents obtained information about the voucher scheme from their children's current providers. The current provider was also the main source of help when parents encountered problems.[3] So for parents whose children were not in a voucher redeeming institution or were not in any provision, it was difficult to receive information and to obtain vouchers. Travellers' families were a particular case here (Unison, September 1996).

Apart from causing confusion and burden for parents, the voucher mechanism also created extra work and additional burden for providers. As a supervisor of a pre-school in Norfolk said, it was 'hard work' for them to understand the voucher booklet (*Nursery World*, 21 March 1996). After understanding the booklet themselves they had to explain it to parents and answer enquiries from them. Explaining to parents would be an on-going task as every year there would be new parents of four-year-olds. Many headteachers or headstaff had to be involved to explain to parents why children needed vouchers (Unison, September 1996). It was also hard work for providers to find out what the 'desirable outcomes' for early years learning exactly meant. Many providers had to revise their policy documents in order to suit the requirements of the 'desirable outcomes' (*Nursery World*, 21 March 1996). Furthermore, it was not easy to gather vouchers from parents due to their insufficient understanding of the voucher scheme. Well after the beginning of the summer term, there were still parents who had not received an application form or had not made an application. There were other parents who had lost their vouchers or had forgotten to hand them in (see DfEE, 1996d). The burden on early years workers was exacerbated in Phase Two when the DfEE issued a list of checks for providers. One of these checks asked providers to rub the vouchers between the thumb and forefinger to check for forgery. Body heat would turn the words 'nursery education' from pink to off-white if the vouchers were genuine. Some cold-fingered staff found that even determined rubbing failed to produce the required effect (see *The Independent*, 10 March 1997).

As a national policy programme, the arrangements of the voucher scheme did not take into consideration the specific circumstances of individual providers. A pre-school in a suburban area of Norfolk faced cash flow difficulties in the period between collecting the vouchers and redeeming them (*Nursery World*, 21 March 1996). Small providers with few assets were likely to face such a problem. Also, vouchers were to be used during term time only. They could not be used in the summer holidays even if some were left over. However, some providers like a private nursery in Norwich did not work termly. The nursery could not afford financially to hold empty places over the summer. They would not be able to accept children who would only attend the nursery during term time (Ibid.).

Despite the problems caused for parents and providers, the resources of the government ensured the relatively smooth running of the voucher scheme. The crucial resources included the organisational resources of a vast administrative apparatus of the civil service, and the financial resources made available for administration and publicity. The DfEE held extensive information campaigns for parents and providers. There were 'the distribution of information leaflets to parents and providers; local press, poster and radio advertising; leaflets in supermarkets, post offices, retail outlets and other centres; ... and telephone information lines for parents and providers' (DfEE, 1996d, p. 10). Two key leaflets were *Nursery Education Voucher Scheme: Information for Parents* and *Nursery Education Vouchers: Questions Parents have been Asking*. The former set out the basis of the scheme. The latter sought to answer some specific questions parents had been asking of providers. There was also publicity in local areas organized by local authorities supported by central government funding.

After recognizing that parents did not sufficiently understand the voucher scheme, the DfEE arranged additional publicity. In particular, all subsequent information material stressed the requirement for vouchers in LEA-maintained settings (AMA, June 1996, p. 15). Some leaflets were made available in up to nine languages with the purpose of reaching non-English speaking families. Also, an arrangement was made to help more vulnerable parents who might not receive information about the scheme to obtain vouchers. Headteachers were given extra application forms to apply for vouchers on behalf of parents in exceptional circumstances (Ibid., p. 18). This meant teachers could apply for vouchers for a pupil who wanted to attend the school but did not have a voucher. Such an arrangement was actually a violation of the free-market principle of the voucher scheme.

Given all the publicity and contingency arrangements, 91 per cent of eligible parents applied for and received vouchers in the summer term of Phase One (HC, March 1997, p. xv). This equated to a coverage composed of 70 per cent of four-year-olds in Kensington and Chelsea, 96 per cent in Wandsworth, 74 per cent in Westminster and 97 per cent in Norfolk (DfEE, 1996d, p. 27). The total application rate increased slightly to 93 per cent in the autumn term (HC, March 1997, p. xv). Those who did not apply for vouchers gave the reasons that the provider which their child attended was not in the scheme; they had only recently moved into the area; or they thought their child was not eligible (DfEE, 1996d, p. 50). Among those parents who had vouchers issued to them, 91 per cent had used the vouchers to exchange for pre-school education in the summer term. This figure was composed of a rate of 95 per cent in Kensington and Chelsea, 88 per cent in Wandsworth, 81 per cent in Westminster and 93 per cent in Norfolk (DfEE, 1996d, p. 27). Parents who did not redeem vouchers gave the reasons that the provider did not accept vouchers; they were unsure how to use the vouchers; or they thought that vouchers were not worth using.

Some parents only redeemed part of the vouchers. Of these, some felt that 2-3 sessions a week were sufficient and preferred to have their child at home at other times. Others found not enough sessions were available or that places were not available (Ibid., p. 50).

With regard to the participation of providers, in the summer term of Phase One, 77 per cent of the private and voluntary providers in Kensington and Chelsea registered to join the voucher scheme. In Wandsworth, 74 per cent of the private and voluntary providers registered. In Westminster, 71 per cent did so, and in Norfolk, 89 per cent (Unison, September 1996). Too much paper work and having no four-year-olds in the establishment were reasons given by private and voluntary providers who did not participate (NCB, 1998, p. 42). Vouchers were not necessary since their parents were well-off was another reason (*Nursery World*, 21 March 1996). All public sector providers joined the scheme. They had no choice about joining as an authority-wide decision was made by their local councils to participate.

A major problem which appeared was the competition between LEA-maintained schools and independent pre-schools for voucher bearing pupils. As discussed in chapter 5, local authorities and pre-schools were both important providers of pre-school education. They both were seen as having the organisational resources that were crucial for the implementation of the voucher scheme. They both gained concessions from the central government in exchange for their resources. As providers of pre-school education, both local authorities and pre-schools would benefit from the voucher money through taking in voucher-bearing four-year-olds. They were in the position of competing with each other since if one took in more voucher-bearing pupils the other would have to take in less. They were both actively involved in the implementation stage in order to ensure a high rate of in-take of such pupils. Local authorities had been unhappy about the arrangement that money had to be re-couped from their SSA to fund the voucher scheme. Their rule was one to protect their own interests against financial lost. They carried out publicity campaigns and worked closely with their schools and parents in order to gain the money back.

Pre-schools had welcomed the voucher scheme as this was the first time they would benefit from public funding as part of a national early years programme (see chapter 5). During the implementation stage, the PLA actively promoted the scheme to their members. Their rule was one to uphold the interests of their member pre-schools. They held a substantial number of seminars and meetings with their county sub-committees and local pre-schools to explain to them the mechanism of the voucher scheme and to encourage members to participate. They also produced publications to prepare members to take part. These included 'Nursery Vouchers: What Do They Mean for Your Pre-school?' (PLA, 1996a), 'Nursery Education Voucher Initiative: Briefing for Sub-Committees' (PLA, 1996b), and 'Nursery Vouchers: Preparing for Inspection' (PLA, 1996c).

At the beginning of Phase One, in the summer term, in response to the new public funding made available through the vouchers, about 41 per cent of pre-schools expanded their premises or increased their number of sessions.[4] In Norfolk, some 1,300 children attended more sessions and an additional 285 children were admitted (although this only averaged out at about one child per setting). However, from the autumn term onwards, some pre-schools closed down and some reduced the number of sessions they offered since many four-year-olds transferred to schools in the maintained sector. New nursery units in schools were built in Norfolk using the extra grant from the DfEE. Most importantly, some schools changed their admission policy and lowered the age at which they would admit pupils to four. Some maintained schools even warned parents that they could not keep places open unless children started at four (*TES*, 31 May 1996). In a PLA survey of their members, 57 per cent of the respondents in Norfolk said their local schools (representing 39 schools) had changed their admission policy. In the London boroughs, 35 per cent of the respondents said so (HC, March 1997, p. xli). Another survey conducted in Norfolk revealed that 29 per cent of the respondents in the independent sector felt they were adversely affected by the expansion of the maintained sector. Five per cent considered themselves in danger of closing by September 1996, and nine per cent thought they would close within the next year (DfEE, 1996d, p. 57).

The problem of competition between maintained schools and pre-schools was worse in Phase Two. In Phase One, the four local authorities volunteered to take part. They worked closely with the DfEE to try out the vouchers. They did not encourage their schools to change admission policy in order to take in more voucher-bearing four-year-olds, although some of their schools had done so. However, all local authorities, the majority of which had reservations about the voucher scheme, had to take part in Phase Two. All they wanted was to get back the money which they lost to fund the vouchers. As a local councillor commented,

We opposed it ... We lobbied against it ... In the end it was implemented. What we then did, we maximized our income from the vouchers. We lost money. We lost millions of pounds as local governments ... We had to maximize our money back. (Interview D)

In a telephone survey of the 115 LEAs in England conducted by the

PLA, only 13 per cent indicated that they would commit to a policy of admitting children to school in the term they become five (HC, March 1997, p. xli). The majority of the LEAs had changed their admission policy to take four-year-olds into reception classes by September 1996, well before Phase Two began. Many local authorities and their schools put pressure on parents, most commonly by suggesting that if a four-year-old did not join the school, no place would be guaranteed when the child became five. In Suffolk, a council official wrote to parents asking them to use vouchers at local schools. Otherwise, the letter said, 'there will not be enough money to pay for teachers, books and everything else' (quoted in *The Times*, 14 March 1997). A school in West Sussex sent letters to parents warning that children could be at a disadvantage unless they joined at the age of four (see Ibid.).

Although the admission of younger children into schools (reception classes) had been a growing trend for some years (see chapter 3), the voucher scheme exacerbated the situation. The early admission of four-year-olds into schools put independent providers, especially small scale pre-schools, under strain. The PLA predicted that 800 pre-schools, especially those in rural areas, faced the danger of closing within the first year of the nationwide operation of the voucher scheme (*The Times*, 14 March 1997). However, despite their protests, the PLA and member pre-schools were not able to make a change to the situation. Local authorities were located at the periphery of the state and had the authority to regulate under-fives services in their local areas. They had control over more crucial resources than the pre-schools and thus were more powerful. The PLA and member pre-schools were not able to intervene in the actions and decisions of local authorities and their schools.

The participation of other interested actors in this policy stage was mainly in the form of monitoring the implementation of the voucher scheme. A number of reports were published as a result.[5] One of the studies was carried out by the Daycare Trust, on behalf of Unison. The purpose of the project was to assess the impact of the voucher scheme (Phase One) upon Unison members and the services they provided to the under-fives. The resulting report, *Inside the Voucher Scheme*, was published in September 1996. Two other monitoring projects were carried out by the Early Childhood Unit of the NCB. The first one was a small-scale study commissioned by the AMA at the beginning of Phase One. Information was sought from local authorities and Capita Managed Services on the initial running of the scheme. The results were published in June 1996 in the report, *Education Vouchers for Early Years: the State of Play*. The second project intended to monitor the scheme over the 12 months of Phase One. Interviews were held with local authorities, providers, providers organizations, parents and nursery inspectors. The report, *Learning from Vouchers: An Evaluation of Phase One of the Four Year Old Voucher Scheme 1996/7*, was ready at the beginning of 1997. The House of Commons Education and Employment Committee also monitored the implementation. They carried out detailed enquiries with the actors who participated in the voucher scheme. The report, *The Operation of the Nursery Education Voucher Scheme*, was published in March 1997. All these reports pointed out the problem of competition between the maintained sector and the independent sector. They raised doubt about whether the voucher scheme would fulfil its aims of expanding provision, improving quality and enhancing parental choice.

Despite the problems raised, no major change was made as a result of the pilot exercise. Some changes made in Phase Two were of a technical nature. The procedure for redeeming vouchers was simplified. No separate claim was required at half term, and no list of names needed to accompany the vouchers. In order to allow more time for applications, information packs were sent to providers and parents two months earlier than in Phase One. A new guide was distributed to explain to parents the main features of different types of provision and to help parents choose between them. Needless to say, no change was made to the core components of the voucher scheme. The core components were decided upon in the earliest policy stages by the leading members of the government who did not participate directly in implementation. The lower ranking minister responsible for implementation was only given the job of making the voucher idea become a reality. He was not powerful enough to make changes to the core components. Therefore, implementation had little effect on policy decision making and hence on the form of the policy initiative. The central state actors largely retained their autonomy in policy making.

Achieving the Aims of the Voucher Scheme?

After looking at the implementation of the voucher scheme, I want to examine how well the scheme achieved its aims. As argued in chapter 4, the decision to use a voucher scheme to expand pre-school education provision for the four-year-olds was influenced by the ideology of the right-wing members of the Conservative Government to develop markets for public provision. They thought that by giving parents of every four-year-old vouchers to exchange for pre-school education in either the public or the independent sector, the scheme would encourage the development of the independent sector. It would then create a market for pre-school education provision. Competition between providers for voucher bearing pupils would distinguish the good quality providers from the bad quality ones. The good ones would thrive, helped by the voucher money, whereas the bad ones would be left to decline. The increased demand for places would create a market force to drive up provision. Therefore, a voucher scheme would enhance both the quality and the quantity of provision. It would thus enhance parental choice. However, evidence suggests that the voucher scheme did not achieve its designated aims.

First and foremost, it is inconclusive as to whether the scheme led to expansion in provision.[6] As stated earlier, the immediate expansion of pre-schools was followed by a reduction when the four-year-olds transferred to schools with the latter's early admission policy. Also, in the Phase One area of Norfolk, although 832 part-time nursery class places were created in the maintained sector, the voucher scheme alone may not have brought about the change. The increase was in the context of Norfolk County Council's previous decision to expand pre-school provision. The voucher scheme helped to bring forward the policy, especially with a grant of one million pounds from the DfEE. Indeed, this was the reason for the Council taking part in Phase One. In Phase Two, there was no extra capital money available for local authorities. Most expansion took the form of early entry of four-year-olds into reception classes in schools. As mentioned in chapter 5, reception classes were subject to lighter regulation than other pre-school settings. There was no statutory requirement for their adult-child ratio. Consequently they usually had a much smaller adult-child ratio and a much larger class size. Although staff were mainly qualified teachers, they often did not have training for teaching the under-fives. It was widely considered that reception classes were not a suitable form of provision for children of such a young age.

It is also inconclusive as to whether the voucher scheme enhanced the quality of provision. A competitive free market was not created (also see later discussion) with the pressure on parents to put their four-year-olds into maintained schools. Thus there was no free market force to separate the good providers from the bad ones, and hence to ensure quality. Additional measures were introduced to ensure quality. As explained earlier, providers were asked to fill in a self-assessment schedule to check whether they would meet the requirements for initial validation. They had to agree to work towards the desirable outcomes for early years learning set out by the SCAA and to be inspected. An additional layer of inspection by Ofsted was introduced to assess the educational provision of private and voluntary institutions. This was carried out by Ofsted Registered Nursery Inspectors (RgNIs) who were to check that the desirable learning outcomes were being actively promoted. However, the evidence raises doubt as to whether these additional measures ensured a good quality of provision.[7]

First of all, after gaining initial validation, settings were allowed to operate up to a year before being inspected. There was wide criticism that such an arrangement could hardly ensure good quality provision. Regarding the desirable learning outcomes, childcare and education specialists generally thought it represented only a minimal statement of what young children should achieve. Also, it required quality staff to deliver quality education, but no steps were taken to improve the insufficient opportunity and resources for the training of under-fives workers. Furthermore, the Unison report on the impact of the voucher scheme upon its members showed that information regarding the learning outcomes had not been disseminated effectively among under-fives workers. None of the staff interviewed had been given the opportunity to study the SCAA document, nor had received training on the subject (Unison, September 1996).

Three hundred RgNIs were recruited in Phase One for the additional layer of inspection. There was concern as to whether the qualifications and training of the RgNIs were sufficient. Attention was drawn to the fact that the quality of the English used in the inspection reports varied widely. There were grammatical mistakes and use of technical language which would not be easily understood by some parents. It was also doubtful whether the inspections were adequate as they were only carried out by one inspector for two and a half hours in each setting. Even with these rather questionable inspection arrangements, the result of the inspections showed that the standard of the independent settings varied widely. Almost half of the settings inspected had weaknesses and needed to be re-inspected within one or two years (see *The Independent*, 19 February 1997). Sixty per cent of the settings had weaknesses in geography, history and science. One in four had weaknesses in mathematics and one in five in literacy. In spite of these findings, only two nurseries were rejected formal validation. All of the others were allowed to operate despite the weaknesses. In addition, reception classes which came under school inspections were not inspected by RgNIs. While four-year-olds were dashing into reception classes, the quality of educational provision for young children there was not ensured.

While it is questionable as to whether the voucher scheme enhanced the quality and the quantity of provision, it is inconclusive as to whether it enhanced parental choice. For less well-off parents whose children did not have a publicly-funded place and had struggled to send them for a few sessions a week to private nurseries or voluntary pre-schools, vouchers enabled their children to have extra sessions at no cost to them. However, parents would only have a choice when there were sufficient places available. For a nursery which already had a long waiting list (such as a nursery centre in Westminster), it simply would not be the case that people could just choose to go there with their vouchers (see *Nursery World*, 21 March 1996). Parental choice was certainly not enhanced when maintained schools brought pressure to bear on parents to put children into schools early. In most of the cases four-year-olds were put into reception classes where the provision was seen as not suitable for children of such a young age. Meanwhile, independent settings were closing down or reducing the number of sessions offered as they lost four-year-olds to the maintained sector. This not only affected the choice of the parents of four-year-olds, but also adversely affected the provision for the three-year-olds in those settings. The three-year-olds left behind lost the opportunity to benefit from learning alongside the four-year-olds (*TES*, 31 May 1996).

Parental choice was further affected by the pressure to bring down the cost per child to the level of 1,100 pounds of the vouchers. This pressure caused the reduction in funding of nursery schools in the maintained sector, or in some cases, closure. Separate nursery schools were more expensive to run than nursery classes or reception classes in schools. This was due to the cost of having a headteacher and of meeting the requirement for a lower adult-child ratio. In Wandsworth, plans to cut 15,000 pounds from the budgets of each of its nursery schools to bring costs more into line with nursery classes were discussed, although they were rejected. Hammersmith and Fulham, which was not in Phase One, made plans to cut budgets in three nursery schools. Another nursery school would be closed down and children there would be allocated to nursery classes in three different schools (*TES*, 3 May 1996).

Apart from not achieving the aims of enhancing quality, quantity and parental choice, the voucher scheme also did not succeed in encouraging the development of the independent sector. Some private settings with well-off parents did not consider vouchers as necessary, while many pre-schools were driven out of business by the competition with the maintained sector. Contrary to developing the independent sector, the voucher scheme actually encouraged the expansion of the maintained sector in the form of reception classes.

The lack of development of the independent sector meant that a free market for pre-school education provision was not created. Some changes made in response to the demand of local authorities before or during the implementation stage also violated the principle of a free market. It was mentioned in chapter 5 that a concession was made to Phase One local authorities so that they received the income from the vouchers instead of it going directly to their schools as originally planned. After negotiation, this arrangement was extended in Phase Two to include all local authorities. This measure allowed local authorities to distribute the money to their schools based on the LMS formula as they did before the voucher scheme was introduced. As a consequence, many authorities paid grants to their schools in advance against the projected number of pupils. This was in contradiction to the free market principle of the voucher scheme, in which funding should be paid to schools based on the number of vouchers received. Furthermore, as mentioned earlier, headteachers were given extra application forms to apply for vouchers on behalf of parents in exceptional circumstances. Headteachers, in effect, could apply for vouchers for those pupils who wanted to attend the school but did not have vouchers. This was also against the principle of a free market. In addition, as parental choice was not enhanced (see previous discussion), the idea that parents as consumers could use vouchers to 'purchase' pre-school education in the market wherever they preferred did not work out.

The outcome of the voucher scheme was not what the leading members of the government, who were responsible for the form of the scheme, had wanted. They did not have control over some resources that were crucial for implementation. They had to rely upon the organizational resources of providers of pre-school education, and the authoritative resources of local authorities, to carry out the policy initiative. Consequently they did not have control over the outcome of implementation. Resource dependency deprived them of the autonomy to achieve the designated aims of the scheme.

It is worth mentioning that the outcome of the voucher scheme was predicted by actors in society and at the periphery of the state in the earlier stages of the policy process before the scheme was implemented (see chapters 4 and 5). They had long argued that the vouchers would lead to no net increase in provision, no enhancement of parental choice, extra burden for providers and competition between sectors. Their opinion was then ignored. Their attempts to influence policy decision making were not successful. The central state actors formulated the policy initiative with a high degree of autonomy and largely according to their own rules. The consequence of their autonomy in policy making was to fail to achieve the aims of the voucher scheme. The opportunity to expand under-fives provision in order to aid women's employment prospects was also missed.

Replacing the Vouchers: Transference of Resources and Power

Despite the apparent failure of the voucher scheme in achieving its aims, it continued to run. The DfEE argued that the aims of the scheme were long term, and that its effect could not be seen in a year or so. Indeed the scheme would have kept running if the Conservative Party had not lost power in the General Election on the First of May 1997. The General Election came only one month after the start of the nationwide operation of the voucher scheme. The vouchers did not become a vote winner for the Conservative Party as thought by the then Prime Minister John Major. Together with the general unpopularity of their policies among the electorate, the Conservatives suffered a historic defeat. The Labour Party won the General Election with a huge majority. They had indicated well before the election that they would scrap the voucher scheme if they gained office (*TES*, 22 November 1996). A week after the election, Labour education ministers started to work on ways to terminate the voucher scheme.

The Labour Party had always opposed the voucher scheme. They had protested against it since the earliest stages of the policy process. They sought to defeat the legislation or make amendments to it during the legislation stage. Labour controlled local authorities boycotted the scheme by not joining Phase One. The Labour-controlled local authority organizations also had campaigned against it all along. The AMA proposed an alternative plan which was discussed in Parliament and by the DfEE. However, despite all their efforts, the Labour Party did not succeed in either stopping the voucher scheme from going ahead or making changes to its core components. They, as Opposition, did not have the crucial resources in policy making which would allow them the capacity to do so.

On the contrary, the dominant members of the Conservative Party, as leading members of the government, occupied the most central and prestigious positions in the state political system through the winning of a General Election. Their prominent positions gave them access to and control over centralized resources. Using their resources they were able to exercise power over other state actors or society actors. They enjoyed a high degree of autonomy in the formulation of the voucher scheme. They made the respective decisions concerning the scheme drawing upon their own rules, i.e. their values, beliefs, ideologies and interests. However, upon losing the subsequent General Election they also lost the crucial resources and hence the autonomy in policy making. The occupation of the most prominent positions was transferred to the dominant members of the winning Labour Party, who gained control over the crucial resources and hence the power to act autonomously in policy decision making. After gaining office, Labour ministers immediately replaced the voucher scheme in accordance with their preferred plan. This had been impossible when they were in opposition, no matter how hard they had campaigned against the voucher scheme.

The plan to replace the vouchers was announced in late May.[8] It was largely based on the alternative proposal suggested by the AMA. The

Labour Government set out to abolish the voucher scheme from September 1997. Local authorities were then expected to draw up 'early years development plans' to explain the steps they would take to develop pre-school education provision for every four-year-old in their areas. The development plans had to be made based on the co-operation and coordination between parents, LEAs, and providers in the private and voluntary sectors through the establishment of an early years forum. Local authorities whose development plans were approved by the government would receive 336 pounds per term for every four-year-old (same as the amount of voucher money). The authorities would then pass the money on to those private or voluntary providers included in the development plan to cover their costs. The development plans would be fully in place from April 1998. During the interim period between September 1997 to April 1998, local authorities which were unable to submit development plans in time could choose not to do so. In those cases, parents whose four-year-olds were in private or voluntary provision could apply to the DfEE for a 'certificate'. This 'certificate' had all the characteristics of a voucher — with five parts each exchangeable for a session of at least 2.5 hours of pre-school education per week for a term. Parents were free to top up the value of the 'certificate'.

The new policy initiative of the Labour Government included many features of the voucher scheme. Public funding was made available for the provision of pre-school education but not daycare. Publicly-funded pre-school education was provided for four-year-olds in preference to three-year-olds or younger children. Funding was made at the level of 1,100 pounds per child, the same as the value of the vouchers. Also, childminders were excluded from receiving public money designated for pre-school education. In this way, the undesirable elements of the voucher scheme continued to influence the form of a later policy. In addition, the trend of four-year-olds going early to reception classes in maintained schools which was exacerbated by the scheme was irreversible. Most importantly, the efforts and work of early years workers in implementing the voucher scheme could not be repaid. All went to waste with the termination of the scheme.

Conclusion

This chapter looked at the last two policy stages of 'implementation' and 'replacement' of the Nursery Education Voucher Scheme. The voucher scheme with its core components was tried in the four volunteer local authorities in Phase One and implemented nationwide a year later. A complicated mechanism of nine procedures was involved. This caused confusion and a burden for parents. It also created an extra work load for early years workers. Despite the problems which appeared, the organisational and financial resources of the government ensured the relatively smooth running of the scheme. Local authorities and pre-schools, which were important providers of pre-school education, participated extensively in this implementation stage. Their competition for voucher-bearing four-year-olds and hence voucher money was apparent. Many LEA-maintained schools introduced an early admission policy to lower the age at which they would admit pupils to four years-old. This adversely affected the existence of providers in the independent sector, especially small scale pre-schools. The participation of other interested actors in the implementation stage was mainly in the form of monitoring the running of the voucher scheme. Despite their substantial criticisms, only a small number of changes of a technical nature were made as a result of the pilot scheme. The central state actors, in effect, largely retained their autonomy in policy making.

Evidence to support the claim that the voucher scheme had achieved its designated aims was inconclusive. Some expansion in the public sector was accompanied by the closing down of some pre-schools and a reduction in the number of sessions in others. Most expansion in the maintained sector was in the form of reception classes where provision was seen as not suitable for young children. The measures to ensure quality were either inadequate or not effectively enacted. Parental choice was not enhanced with insufficient places available, the pressure to put four-year-olds into maintained schools, and the need to bring down the cost per child to the level of the vouchers. A free market for pre-school education provision was not created. Whereas the scheme did not encourage the development of the independent sector, it enhanced the expansion of the maintained sector. Some concessions made to local authorities also violated the principle of a free market.

The outcome of the voucher scheme was not what the leading members of the Conservative Government, who were responsible for the form of the scheme, had wanted. However, they were unable to influence the outcome. They did not have control over the organisational resources of providers of pre-school education which were crucial for implementing the scheme. Resource dependency deprived them of autonomy in achieving the aims of the policy initiative. Those who had the crucial organisational resources were pre-schools and local authorities. Of these, local authorities had more crucial resources than pre-schools since they had the authority to regulate under-fives provision in their local areas. Local authorities were the most influential in implementation.

Despite the apparent failure of the voucher scheme in achieving its aims, it would have continued if the Conservative Party had not lost the 1997 General Election. With their election defeat, the dominant members of the Conservative Party lost the prominent positions they occupied. These positions were transferred to the dominant members of the winning Labour Party. The Conservatives' control over the crucial resources and their power to act autonomously in policy making was also transferred to Labour. With their new autonomy, Labour ministers wasted no time in replacing the voucher scheme.

The voucher scheme was formulated based on the rules of the dominant members of the ruling Conservative Party who, as the leading members of the then Conservative Government, had a high degree of autonomy in policy making. The policy initiative which was formulated in such a narrow sense did not achieve the immediate aims of those central state actors. More importantly, it moved far away from the demand in society for more childcare facilities to aid women's employment prospects. The unpopularity of the voucher scheme did not allow it to survive the change of government and transference of power. The efforts of early years workers in implementing the voucher scheme were wasted. While the scheme itself did not survive, many of its undesirable elements continued to have an impact on later under-fives policy and provision.

Notes

1   Eligible parents here refer to parents and legal guardians in the four local authority areas in Phase One, whose children would reach the age of four before the coming summer term. They were identified from the CBC database.

2   The NVC was the body responsible for the issuing and redemption of vouchers. It was operated by Capita Managed Services, a private company which won the contract from the DfEE to administer the scheme (HC, 1997, p. xiii). In Phase Two, the NVC had access to the CBC data. It sent application forms directly to parents.

3   DfEE, 1996d; Unison, September 1996.

4   DfEE, 1996d; HC, March 1997.

5   All the major reports are used as references for the discussion in this chapter.

6   Also see DfEE, 1996d, p. 56; HC, March 1997, pp. xxiv - xxvi, xliv; NCB, 1998, chapter 4 and pp. 169 - 171; Unison, September 1996, p. 5.

7   See HC, March 1997, pp. xxvii - xxxvii, xiv - xlvi; Unison, September 1996, pp. 5 - 6.

8   For the Labour Government's plan to replace the vouchers, also see *The Independent*, 7 May 1997; *TES*, 16 May 1997; *The Telegraph*, 23 May 1997; *Nursery World*, 29 May 1997; *TES*, 30 May 1997.

7 Conclusion

The book started by raising the concern of insufficient public childcare provision in Britain, and contesting that this adversely affected the attainment of equal citizenship rights for women. It set out to search for the crucial factors that constrained the development of childcare policy and public childcare provision. It considered that a systematic analysis of the policy process was necessary for this purpose. The study is significant in the sense that women-centred policy has been a marginal interest among scholars of the policy process and policy making. The study will fill in some of the gaps in the literature.

The book identified two dimensions to the analysis of the policy process — the 'actors' and the 'process'. The 'process' dimension was concerned with the dynamic process of policy making. This process was separated into some highly related but distinct stages. Each of the stages had a different function in the policy process and different implications for policy outcomes. Each required independent and detailed analysis. The 'actors' dimension focused on the participation of policy actors who sought to influence policy decision making. The analysis within this dimension was concerned with three questions. Firstly, who were the policy actors? Secondly, what were their actions and decisions? Thirdly, why did they take such actions and make these decisions? There were three further aspects to understanding this last question. Firstly, what were the rules (values, beliefs, ideologies and interests) actors drew upon for their actions and decisions? Secondly, what was the influence of previous policy on actors' actions and decisions? Thirdly, what were the relationships of resource dependency between policy actors, and how did these relationships affect policy outcomes?

Through the analysis of the policy process, I set out to consider the relevance of existing theories of the state to the empirical reality of childcare policy making. These theories included Marxism, pluralism and state autonomy. Marxism argues that policy is made according to either the need of the capitalist economy or the interests of the capitalists. Pluralism argues that policy making is the result of political participation and pressure of a large number of interest groups. Theorists of state autonomy argue that state actors make policy according to their own policy preferences in order to achieve their own goals, i.e. they have autonomy in policy making.

The policy initiative studied in detail in this book was the Nursery Education Voucher Scheme introduced in the latter half of the 1990s. The reason for choosing this policy initiative was that it involved, at that time, the largest ever amount of public money allocated to childcare provision. However it failed to achieve the immediate goal of providing pre-school education for all four-year-olds. The adoption of the policy initiative also missed the opportunity to expand public childcare provision in those forms which would have assisted women with paid work participation.[1]

In this concluding chapter, I summarize the crucial factors that influenced the form of the voucher scheme identified during the course of the study of its policy process. The discussion will reveal the elements that constrained the attainment of equal citizenship rights for women. It will also point out the relevance of the theoretical stances of Marxism, pluralism and state autonomy to the empirical reality of childcare policy making. The rest of the chapter reflects on the analytical schema set out for the study and considers the measures which would lead to policy making being more responsive to social demand. It includes a rethinking of the phenomenon of state autonomy, its implications for the representative democratic state of governance and the rights of the citizen.

The Deciding Factors

In studying the policy process of the Nursery Education Voucher Scheme, a complicated picture appears with regard to the crucial factors which influenced policy making. It is apparent, though, that a distinction can be made between two levels of decisions — 'higher level' decisions and 'lower level' decisions. 'Higher level' decisions are those decisions relating to the core components of the voucher scheme. 'Lower level' decisions are those decisions relating to the technical details of the policy initiative.

The 'higher level' decisions were made in the earlier stages of the policy process, including 'agenda setting', 'option selection' and 'legislation'. In the stage of 'agenda setting', the decision was made to put the provision of part-time pre-school education for all four-year-olds onto the policy agenda. In the stage of 'option selection', a universal voucher scheme was chosen to make the provision. In the stage of 'legislation', the voucher scheme with its core components gained legitimacy to go ahead. In these earlier stages, the leading members of the government, including the Prime Minister, ministers from the Treasury Office and other right-wing ministers, were directly involved. The respective decisions on the core components of the voucher scheme were made according to their policy preferences in order to achieve their own goals. Hence they had a high degree of autonomy in the making of the 'higher level' decisions. This was possible since they had control over the resources crucial for policy making. These resources included authority, money, information, organisation and legitimacy. The Prime Minister had the authority to oversee the work of the government. The Treasury had the authority to control the use of public money and to regulate the tax system. The right-wing ministers had the organizational resources of party-political support since the right-wing ideology was the dominant ideology of the ruling Conservative Party at that time. In Parliament, these leading members of the government had control over the information concerning the proposed policy initiative which was not explained in full in the Bill and thus was not available to the Opposition. They also had the organizational resources of a majority of MPs in the House of Commons. Such resources were mustered by party whips who ensured government MPs supported the government. In addition, as elected Members of Parliament, they had a higher degree of legitimacy in policy making than the non-elected peers.

After the decisions relating to the core components were made, the leading members of the government did not participate in the later stages of 'policy negotiation' and 'implementation'. The job to make the voucher concept become a reality was given to a lower ranking minister who did not participate in the discussions in the earlier policy stages. Whatever changes he had to make during the negotiations with other actors concerned and during the implementation of the policy initiative, he was not powerful enough to make any change to the core components. In this way, using their authority to allocate responsibilities to lower ranking ministers, the leading members of the government, in effect, secured their autonomy in the making of the 'higher level' policy decisions.

The 'lower level' decisions — decisions relating to the technical details of the policy initiative were made mainly in the later policy stages. Those actors who had the crucial resources that the central state actors needed in order to achieve the latter's own goals were able to influence some of these decisions. In the 'legislation' stage, ministers made a number of changes to the proposed Bill in order to gain enough support from MPs, who had legitimacy to legislate. In the 'policy negotiation' stage, pre-schools, who had the organizational resources crucial for implementing the voucher scheme, and were originally given a half-rate voucher, successfully demanded a full-rate one. Also, the four local authorities who joined Phase One successfully demanded a number of concessions from ministers in exchange for their participation. Local authorities had the organizational resources for implementing the voucher scheme and the authority to regulate under-fives services in their local areas. In the 'implementation' stage in Phase Two, more changes were made in response to local authorities' requests. However, all the changes made were of a technical nature and did not affect the core components of the voucher scheme. In addition, the central state actors had control over the extent of the changes. They had control over the extent of resource exchange and the extent to which they modified their policy preferences to bring them more into line with those of other resourceful actors.

There was no obvious presence of economic or capitalist interests in the policy process, although the concern over the demographic time-bomb was one of the factors which led the Government to pay serious attention to the childcare issue and consider expanding provision. But this economic factor had no effect on the form of the voucher scheme. The type of provision which would enable mothers of young children to take up full-time paid work (full-time daycare which caters for all children younger than five), and hence would be a potential solution to the demographic time-bomb, did not become the focus of policy action.

The presence of pluralist politics was apparent throughout the policy process. Various interested actors sought to influence policy decisions by sending out press releases, writing to the press, writing and talking to ministers, lobbying, organizing demonstrations, participating in official consultation exercises, carrying out research and publishing research reports, etc. However, as stated previously, other than the central state actors, no other actor was able to influence the 'higher level' decisions. Those actors who had the crucial resources that the central state actors needed in order to achieve the latter's own goals were able to influence some of the 'lower level' decisions. Those actors who had no crucial resources had no influence on policy decisions at all.

On the whole, the leading members of the government had a high degree of autonomy in policy making. The voucher scheme, particularly its core components, was influenced by the rules of these central state actors. The most important rules here included the ones to minimize public expenditure, to create a market for the provision of public services, and to enhance the traditional family and motherhood. Previous childcare policy and its consequences had effects on the decisions of the central state actors, and hence on the form of the voucher scheme, too.

Controlling public expenditure has always been a major rule of the governments in Britain. As Mullard puts it,

> The common theme over the past three decades has been that governments need to bring public expenditure under control; that public expenditure has its

own momentum towards increased growth, that it behaves like a super-tanker which is difficult and slow to turn around because of in-built inertia and the influence of many vested interests and that the best-hoped policy is for governments to keep expenditure under control (Mullard, 1995, p. 121).

In the early 1990s when the new policy initiative was under consideration, the need to control public expenditure was reinforced by two other issues. Firstly, public expenditure had been continually expanding. In 1993 it was at 45 per cent of GDP, 6 per cent higher than when the Conservative Party first came to office fourteen years previously (Ibid., p. 120). There was a need to control public expenditure in order to reduce the deficit in the public sector. Secondly, the Government made the reduction of personal taxation its priority as a pre-election sweetener. It was necessary to control public expenditure in order to make room for the tax reduction (see Mullard, 1995). With these needs to control spending, when the Conservative Government had to respond to social demand for more childcare provision, they chose the cheapest option of providing mainly part-time pre-school education for four-year-olds using a universal voucher scheme.

The need to control public expenditure was reinforced by the New Right Ideology to create markets for the provision of public services. Supporters of New Right thinking advocated a radical reform of the welfare state in order to control the size of the public sector and to reduce public expenditure. They argued that the government should privatize a major part of public services, and that there should be limited government involvement in their provision. The leading members of the Conservative Government were distinctly right-wing and supported the ideological principle of creating markets for public provision. They made the decision to use a universal voucher scheme to provide pre-school education for four-year-olds. Public funding was made available through vouchers which were given to parents of every four-year-old to exchange for pre-school education in the private, voluntary or public sector.

The decision to provide mainly part-time pre-school education for four-year-olds was affected by another aspect of the New Right Ideology, that of the traditional family and motherhood. Advocates argued for the enhancement of social order based on traditional social and moral views. They considered the traditional family as an institution important for enhancing social order. For this purpose they believed that mothers should stay at home to bolster the family and care for and educate young children. The leading members of the Conservative Government supported this ideological thinking of enhancing the family and motherhood. They made the decision to provide mainly part-time (2.5 hours a day) pre-school education for four-year-olds (instead of providing full-time daycare, or both care and education, or including younger children). Provision made in this way would do little to encourage mothers of young children to go out to work, certainly not full-time.

The decisions of the central state actors were also affected by childcare policy in the past and the way childcare provision had developed as a consequence. One issue was that childcare policy had given separate consideration to care and education for the under-fives. This enabled the option of making provision for pre-school education to be adopted in preference to a provision that would involve the element of care. Historically pre-school education was mainly part-time and for older pre-school children (three- and four-year-olds). The provision of care, however, was full-time and for younger children as well. Making provision for pre-school education would be cheaper. This was in line with the rule of controlling public expenditure. This was also in agreement with the rule of enhancing the traditional family and motherhood, since it would do little to encourage mothers of young children to go out to work.

Another issue was that previous childcare policy had been reluctant to develop provision in the public sector. The demand for childcare facilities had led to a significant and continual growth of the private and voluntary sectors. When the new policy initiative was under consideration, it was obvious that the limited facilities in the public sector were not enough to cater for all four-year-olds. At the time 19 per cent of four-year-olds were in some form of independent provision. Making use of the facilities available in the private and voluntary sectors would lessen the burden on the government to create new places. This was in line with the rule of controlling public expenditure. This was also compatible with the rule of creating markets for the provision of public services. Consequently, publicly-funded vouchers were to be used to exchange for pre-school education in the private and voluntary sectors, as well as the public sector.

With the influence of the rules of the central state actors and past policy, the very conception of the voucher scheme was in contradiction with the achievement of equal citizenship rights for women. Since the provision was mainly part-time and for four-year-olds only, the scheme did not encourage women with young children to go out to work, certainly not full-time. This constrained women in the attainment of the social right to economic welfare by wage-earning through paid work. The scheme consequently disadvantaged women in the welfare system, since under the contributory principle of the system, entitlements to welfare benefits are linked to contributions through paid work (also see chapter 1). The policy initiative also did not help women to achieve the right to political participation. Women who were bound by childcare responsibilities and could not participate in paid work were unlikely to have the time and money to participate in politics (see Ibid.). It is worth recalling that the policy in the past was also influenced by similar rules of the then central state actors. So as long as these rules remain the ideologies and beliefs of the most powerful central state actors, it is unlikely that childcare policy would fully support the achievement of broader citizenship rights for women.

The voucher scheme, which was in the main the result of the autonomy of the central state actors in policy making, was unable to achieve its immediate goal of expanding pre-school education provision for all four-year-olds. It was also unsuccessful in achieving the aims of ensuring quality, enhancing parental choice, encouraging the development of the independent sector and creating a market for pre-school education provision. Such an outcome was not what the central state actors had wanted. However, they did not have autonomy in seeking to achieve the aims of the policy initiative in the stage of implementation, since they did not have control over the organizational resources of providers of pre-school education necessary for enacting the voucher scheme. This discrepancy between policy making and enactment in terms of who had the crucial resources and hence were the most influential, resulted in the wasting of public money and the effort of under-fives workers. The policy initiative was unpopular and did not survive a change of government. The Labour Government replaced the voucher scheme soon after their election victory in May 1997.

In view of the failure of the voucher scheme, in the following discussion, I would like to consider the measures that should be taken so that the making of childcare policy becomes more responsive to social demand. The discussion will also reflect on the various elements of the analytical schema which I set out to study the policy process.

The Actors and the Process

Society actors from interest organizations and state actors from political institutions all played important parts in the policy process of the voucher scheme. The political institutions included the Government, government departments (mainly the DfEE), the Civil Service, Parliament and local councils. Interest organizations included childcare interest groups, education interest groups, providers' organizations and right-wing think-tanks. Political parties also had substantial involvement. Among these actors, as discussed previously, the most influential in policy making were the leading members of the government - the central state actors.

With regard to the models of British politics discussed in chapter 2, the case study involved a combination of the party government model and the cabinet government model. I shall call it a cabinet-party government model. Under this model, the central state actors, who were also the dominant members of the ruling party, predominated in policy making. The voucher scheme was formulated in line with the wishes of the party leadership and with the party's values and ideologies. The government department responsible, and ministers and civil servants in that department, had minimal say in determining the form of the policy. They were only accountable for working out the technical details and for dealing with various interested actors in society and at the periphery of the state. The democratic institution of Parliament was ineffective in changing the government's policy proposal. The majority of the interest groups were insignificant in their attempts to influence policy decision making.

Only local authorities and pre-schools, who had the resources crucial for enacting the voucher scheme, successfully demanded a number of changes to the policy initiative in the later stages of 'policy negotiation' and 'implementation'. But these changes were mainly related to the technical details and did not affect the core components. The core components of the voucher scheme were decided upon in the earliest stages of 'agenda setting' and 'option selection' by the leading members of the government. In these early stages, the participation of local councils and interest groups was mainly in the form of expressing opinions through the official consultation exercise and was insignificant in influencing policy decision making. When they had a higher degree of participation in the later stages, the decisions on the core components had already been made and the central state actors had little involvement. The responsibility to negotiate with other resourceful actors was given to a lower ranking minister who was not powerful enough to change the decisions of the leading members of the government. It was then too late to make any change to the core components. Therefore, the study of the policy process in stages suggests that any serious attempt by interested actors (particularly those who have some crucial resources) to influence policy making should be made in the earliest stages of the policy process when the basic form of the policy is still under consideration.

The policy network which evolved among the interested actors had the characteristics of an issue network. There were a large number of participants in the network. They had varied and sometimes conflicting interests. Some actors were interested in childcare provision in general whereas others were only concerned with the educational aspect of the issue. Many actors prioritized the interests of their clients or themselves as recipients of the policy initiative, but the interests of some actors contradicted the interests of others. An obvious case was the conflict in interests between pre-schools and local authorities. Both pre-schools and local authority schools were important providers of pre-school education. They were put in the position of competing with each other since if one took more voucher-bearing pupils, and hence more voucher money, the other would have to take less. Within the policy network, there was also an unequal distribution of resources among the participants. Whereas pre-schools and local authorities had the resources that were crucial for the voucher scheme, other actors had no crucial resources. The varied interests and the unequal distribution of resources resulted in a low degree of interdependence among actors in the network.

The loosely integrated relationships between policy actors as is found in an issue network was not helpful in attempts to influence policy. The presence of many actors with varied interests in effect enhanced the autonomy of the central state actors in policy making. The conflict between the actors who had the crucial resources further weakened the pressure on the central state actors.

The experience of the voucher scheme shows, in order to press effectively a demand on the government, there needs to be a high degree of co-operation between the various interested actors. Those who have the crucial resources need to share their resources with other actors in order to create a powerful opposition force. Alliance is also possible between interested actors and government departments. In this case study, the government department responsible, the DFE, actually disagreed with the policy preferences of the leading members of the government in the earliest stages of the policy process. The policy goals of the DFE were closer to the goals of the actors in society and at the periphery of the state than to the goals of the leading members of the government. The DFE and other interested actors could have formed an alliance to campaign against the central state actors.

Rules, Resources and Previous Policy

In the analysis of why actors make certain actions and decisions (hence policy), I considered that there were three aspects to understand: previous policy, the rules actors draw upon for their actions and decisions, and the relationships of resource dependency between actors. I regarded rules to be the values, beliefs, ideologies and interests of policy actors. The analysis of these four factors is not uncommon in the study of policy making. The same is true for the study of resource dependency. However, the analysis in this study is inspired by Giddens's powerful account of the production of action. Its implication is that values, beliefs or resources alone are not sufficient in explaining policy making. It requires the consideration of the combined effect of the three aspects of rules, resources and previous policy in order to analyse systematically the factors that influence policy.

The course of the study in this book revealed some interesting additional connections between the three elements of rules, resources and previous policy. Regarding the aspect of rules, the leading members of the government were influenced by the belief in the need to control public spending, the ideology of the traditional family and motherhood, and that of market provision of public services. Apart from these rules, the rules that influenced the actions and decisions of the majority of the actors were the interests which they wanted to protect or promote. This resource aspect of rules was very important for actors' actions and decisions. This is not surprising when considering actors rely on resources to survive or function, and resources give actors the capacity to exercise power. So through their attempts to influence policy, actors seek to further promote or protect their interests.

The voucher scheme had features similar to childcare policy in the past. Both involved separate consideration of care and education for the under-fives. Both saw a greater willingness to provide pre-school education, which meant part-time provision for older pre-school children, than to provide daycare, which meant full-time provision for younger children as well. Although the policy in the past had effects on the form of the voucher scheme, the aspects of rules and resources were important in influencing the policy initiative. The most significant rules here included the ideology of motherhood and the family, and the belief in the need to control public expenditure. Both rules led to the preference of expanding pre-school education instead of daycare. This option became policy due to the relationships of resource dependency between actors. Those actors who preferred the option had control over the centralized resources. They were the most depended upon by other actors for resources and were the most powerful in policy making.

Similar sets of rules and similar relationships of resource dependency influenced policy in the past. As discussed in chapter 3, childcare policy of successive Conservative administrations in earlier decades was influenced by the ideology of motherhood and the family, and the belief in the need to control public spending. The last Labour Government (before the voucher scheme) in the 1970s, although not claiming explicitly a similar ideological belief, enacted massive cuts in public expenditure. In addition, the structure of political power, and hence the relationships of resource dependency between policy actors in the political system, had not undergone significant change since the end of the Second World War.

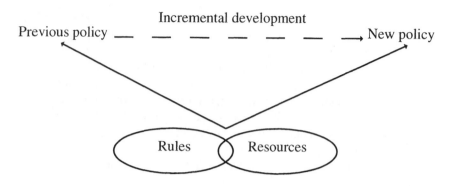

Figure 7.1 Incremental Policy Development and Rules and Resources

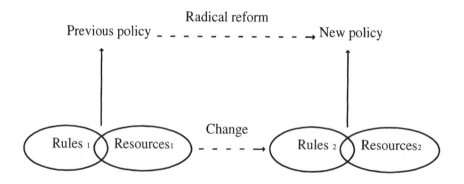

Figure 7.2 Radical Policy Reform and Rules and Resources

Therefore, the similarity of the features of the voucher scheme and those of policy in the past was not only due to the former being influenced by the latter, but also due to the fact that they were influenced by similar sets of rules and similar relationships of resource dependency. This finding is important for understanding the incremental nature of policy development (Figure 7.1).   Any pursuit of radical policy reform would require a fundamental change of either the rules of the most powerful actors, or the relationships of resource dependency between actors and hence the structure of political power, or both (Figure 7.2).

As far as childcare policy is concerned, the making of the policy in a way which would respond to the demands in society needs a fundamental change in the attitude of the leading members of the government towards women and employment, and in their willingness to spend more public money on childcare provision. Or more radically, it requires a reform of the existing power structure in the political system. That is, a reform of the relationship of autonomy and dependency between the central state actors and other policy actors.

State Autonomy and Representative Democracy

The situation of state autonomy, as revealed by the current study, is in contradiction with the system of representative democracy which is espoused by advanced capitalist societies including Britain. Representative democracy is 'a system of rule embracing elected "officers" who undertake to "represent" the interests or views of citizens within delimited territories while upholding the "rule of law"' (Held, 1995, p. 5). It is the key institutional innovation of modern times to overcome the problem of balancing the coercive power of the centre of the state, and the rights and liberty of the citizen. The thinking is that regular elections force a clarification of public issues; the elected few would be competent and accountable to the electorate and do what is best in the public interest (Held, 1995).

The ideal of representative democracy was not achieved in this case study. The influence of the institution of representative democracy — Parliament, was insignificant. Policy making was dominated by the leading members of the government. Policy was not made in the best interests of the public, but to sustain the values, beliefs, ideologies and interests of these dominant members of the ruling party. Thus the system of governance involved what Poulantzas (1978) calls a 'single-party centre'. This institutional feature enhanced the influence of the ruling party and its dominant ideology in policy making. It limited the influence of the popular masses and the political Opposition. As a result, the elected representatives could not 'protect the citizens from the despotic use of political power' (Held, 1995, p. 10) by actors at the centre of the state. The situation was one of 'authoritative statism', as termed by Poulantzas (1978).

The failure of representative democracy and the emergence of authoritative statism deprives citizens of their rights in at least two ways. It deprives citizens of their political right to participate in the exercise of power. It also endangers their social right as receivers of public policy. A member of a community should have the right to exercise political power, either as a member of a body invested with political authority, or as an elector of the members of such a body (Marshall, 1964; also see chapter 1). The elected members of this body exercise political power on behalf of the electorate, and hence make policy according to the wishes of the electorate. However, in the present study, the elected members lacked the capacity to make policy to provide more public childcare in order to meet the demands in society. As a consequence, citizens were deprived of their right to exercise political power. A member of a community should also have the social right to a moderate level of economic welfare and security (Ibid.). This involves the right to work in order to live according to the standards in society. However, in the current study, the introduction of the voucher scheme deprived women of this social right since it failed to enact measures to expand the insufficient public childcare provision, particularly in those forms (full-time daycare which caters for all children younger than five) that would encourage women to take up paid work.

A change in policy in order to promote the rights of the citizen requires the enhancement of representative democracy and the weakening of authoritative statism. This means invalidating the 'single-party centre' and the autonomy of the central state actors in policy making.[2] The main problem here, I consider, lies in the way the most resourceful body — the Government, is formed. In Britain, the political party which wins a simple majority in a General Election has the legitimacy to form a Government. The system of election does not have a direct say on who should become members of the government. The leader of the winning party becomes the Prime Minister. He/she chooses suitable people from their Parliamentary Party (the MPs in their party) to become members of the government. The ones chosen are usually the dominant members of the party and supporters of the party ideology. As members of the government they have control over the centralized resources necessary for policy making (see previous discussions). With these essential resources they enjoy domination in the political system and autonomy in policy making. In this way, the power from the popular masses to govern through the system of representative democracy and election is not given to all the elected, but is accumulated in the hands of the dominant members of the ruling party.

To better fulfil the rights of the citizen, a radical reform of the system of governance would be necessary. Recently there have been some related attempts in Britain by the Labour Government. One attempt has been the reform the system of election and adopt the model of proportional representation for some elections. Indeed, new to British politics, proportional representation was recently used in the elections of the Welsh Assembly and the Scottish Parliament. As a result, a coalition government has been formed in Scotland and a minority government in Wales. Another attempt by the Labour Government has been to include leading members of other political parties in government committees and allow them to participate in the work of the government. These are moves in the right direction, although a more thorough reform would require the decentralisation of resources away from the hands of the leading members of the government and the dominant members of the ruling party. This could be achieved by a number of measures. One such measure would be to bring in more democracy in political parties and encourage 'free votes' in Parliament. Another would be to enhance coalition politics and develop coalition governments from a combination of political parties. There could also be a direct election of key members of the government from candidates of all political parties. The purposes of these measures are to increase the accountability of the government Executive and to diminish the domination of the ruling party.

In practice any such reform would be difficult. With the autonomy of the central state actors, any decision for reform would be made in favour of the ruling party and would work to sustain its domination.[3] However, we see in history a gradual progression in the system of governance, from coercive government to representative democracy, one which is fairer and more democratic. We should be optimistic that a future system of governance will more fully appreciate the rights of the citizen. What would be the components of this future system? This is perhaps a task for social scientists to resolve. Comparative studies of different forms of governance which exist under the umbrella of representative democracy would be essential. The imaginative capacity of the intellectual would be a necessary supplement.

Notes

1   The pursuit of this line of study has resulted in the neglect of other possible issues. Issues which occurred within the childcare sector but had nothing to do with the voucher scheme have not been discussed. Consequently, due to the narrow concern of the scheme (i.e. pre-school education provision for four-year-olds), scant account was given of those childcare interest groups which had little involvement in the issue. They included, for instance, the KCN, which is concerned with after school care; and Parents at Work, which is concerned with helping parents with childcare problems. Hence, no account was given of the childcare network in general. However, to address these issues one would have to adopt a different analytical approach. I doubt that the findings would differ from this study in any significant manner.

2   With regard to this conclusion about the autonomy of the central state actors in policy making, I want to clarify two points. Firstly, I do not suggest that state autonomy is a fixed structural feature of the British state. One case study alone does not warrant such a conclusion. But what this study does suggest is that the British state contains the structural element — the centralised resources in the hands of the leading members of

the government, that enables these central state actors to act autonomously in policy making. Secondly, there is other evidence which supports the argument for the autonomy of the central state actors in policy making. One piece of evidence which immediately comes to mind is the fact that the British Government has only ever lost a government bill a handful of times in Parliamentary history. Other evidence, although indirect, is the low turnout in elections and the general apathy to mainstream politics from large sections of the population (Barnes, *et al.*, 1997) and in connection with this, the mushrooming of informal politics and the growing interest in public involvement in the provision of public services (Barnes, *et al.*, 1997; LGMB, 1997; Lupton, *et al.*, 1998; McIver and Skelcher, 1997; Smith, 1999).

3   An example is the proposed reform of the election system for the General Election previously under consideration by the Labour Government.

Bibliography

Abbott, P. and Wallace, C. (1992), *The Family and the New Right*, Pluto Press, London.

Anderson, J.E. (1975), *Public Policy Making*, Nelson, London.

Ashford, D. (1981), *Policy and Politics in Britain*, Blackwell, Oxford.

Ashford, N. (1993) 'The Ideas of the New Right', in Jordan, G. and Ashford, N. (eds), *Public Policy and the Impact of the New Right*, Pinter Publishers, London and New York.

Association of Metropolitan Authorities (AMA) (1996), *Education Vouchers for Early Years: the State of Play*, AMA, London.

Audit Commission (1996), *Counting to Five*, The Stationery Office, London.

Bachrach, P. and Baratz, M.S. (1970), *Power and Poverty: Theory and Practice*, Oxford University Press, London.

Bagott, R. (1995), *Pressure Groups Today*, Manchester University Press, Manchester.

Baldwin, S. and Falkingham, J. (eds) (1994), *Social Security and Social Change: New Challenges to the Beveridge Model*, Harvester Wheatsheaf, New York.

Barnes, M., Hall, D., Leurs, R., McIver, S. and Stewart, J. (1997), *Citizen Participation: A Framework for Evaluation*, Occasional Paper 11, School of Public Policy, The University of Birmingham, Birmingham.

Becher, J. (1994), *Filling the Gap: Mothers, Work and Child Care for Pre-school Children*, unpublished MA Dissertation, University of Essex.

Bellamy, R. (1999), *Liberalism and Pluralism: Towards a Politics of Compromise*, Routledge, London and New York.

Benson, J.K. (1982), 'A Framework for Policy Analysis', in Rogers, D. *et al.* (eds), *Interorganisational Coordination*, Iowa State University Press, Iowa.

Bramley, M. and Hill, G. (1986), *Analysing Social Policy*, Basil Blackwell, Oxford.

Brennan, D. (1998), *The Politics of Australian Child Care: Philanthropy to Feminism and Beyond*, Revised Edition, Cambridge University Press, Cambridge.

Brown, P. and Sparks, R. (eds) (1989), *Beyond Thatcherism: Social Policy, Politics and Society*, Open University Press, Milton Keynes.

Bryson, V. (1992), *Feminist Political Theory: An Introduction*, Macmillan, London.

Bull, J. *et al.* (1994), *Implementing the Children Act for Children Under 8*, Her Majesty's Stationery Office (HMSO), London.

Burch, M. and Wood, B. (1990), *Public Policy in Britain*, Second Edition, Blackwell, Oxford.

157

Caesar, G. *et al.* (1996), *Early childhood Provision in Britain in the 1990s*, NCB, London.

Central Statistical Office (1996), 'Women in the Labour Market: Results from the Spring 1995 Labour Force Survey', *Labour Market Trends*, March 1996, HMSO, London.

Cohen, B. (1988), *Caring for Children: Services and Policies for Childcare and Equal Opportunities in the United Kingdom*, Report for the European Commission's Childcare Network, Family Policy Studies Centre, London.

Cohen, B. (1990), *Caring for Children: the 1990 Report, Report for the European Commission's Children Network on Childcare Services and Policy in the UK*, Family Policy Studies Centre, London.

Cohen, B and Fraser, N. (1991), *Childcare in a Modern Welfare System*, Institute for Public Policy Research, London.

Cohen, I.J. (1989), *Structuration Theory: Anthony Giddens and the Constitution of Social Life*, Macmillan, London.

Craib, I. (1992), *Anthony Giddens*, Routledge, London.

Davies, B. and Ward, S. (1992), *Women and Personal Pensions*, HMSO, London.

Davis, D. MP (1997), *A Guide to Parliament*, Penguin Books and BBC Books, London.

Daycare Trust (1999a), 'Childcare Gaps', *Childcare Now*, May 1999, Daycare Trust, London.

Daycare Trust (1999b), 'The National Childcare Strategy', *Childcare Now*, May 1999, Daycare Trust, London.

Daycare Trust (1999c), 'What is the National Childcare Strategy?', Briefing Paper, *Childcare Now* (Special Issue), May 1999, Daycare Trust, London.

Department for Education and Employment (DfEE) (1996a), *Nursery Education: Desirable Outcomes for Children's Learning on Entering Compulsory Education*, January 1996, DfEE, London.

DfEE (1996b), *Nursery Education: The Next Steps*, January 1996, DfEE, London.

DfEE (1996c), *Nursery Education Voucher Scheme: A Guide for Parents*, November 1996, DfEE, London.

DfEE (1996d), *Nursery Education Voucher Scheme: Report on Phase 1*, November 1996, DfEE, London.

DfEE (1996e), *Work and Family: Ideas and Options for Childcare*, DfEE, London.

DfEE (1998), *Pupils Under Five Years of Age in Schools in England - January 1997*, DfEE, London.

DfEE (1999), *Statistics of Education: Children's Day Care Facilities at 31 March 1998 England*, DfEE, London.

Department of Health (DoH) (1989), *Children's Day Care Facilities at 31 March 1988*, Government Statistical Service, London.

DoH (1996), *Children's Day Care Facilities at 31 March 1995*, Government Statistical Service, London.

DoH (1998), *Children's Day Care Facilities at 31 March 1997*, Government Statistical Service, London.

DoH (1992), *Playgroups in Practice: Self-help and Public Policy*, HMSO, London.

Dietz, M. (1992), 'Context is All: Feminism and Theories of Citizenship', in

Turner and Hamilton (eds) (1994), *Citizenship: Critical Concepts*, Routledge, London and New York.

Domhoff, G. W. (1996), *State Autonomy or Class Dominance? Case Studies on Policy Making in America*, Aldine de Gruyter, New York.

Dowding, K. (1995), 'Model or Metaphor?: A Critical Review of the Policy Network Approach', *Political Studies*, no. 43, pp. 136-158.

Dunleavy, P., Gamble, A., Holliday, I. and Peele, G. (eds) (1993), *Developments in British Politics*, Fourth Edition, Macmillan, London.

Early Childhood Education Forum (ECEF), *Nursery Education and Grant-Maintained Schools Bill: Briefing for House of Lords second reading*, April 1996, ECEF, London.

Easton, D. (1965), *A Systems Analysis of Political Life*, John Wiley and Sons, New York and London.

Elshtain, J.B. (1981), *Public Man, Private Woman*, Martin Robertson, Oxford.

Esping-Andersen, G. (1990), *The Three Worlds of Welfare Capitalism*, Polity Press, Cambridge.

Evans, P. (1995), *Embedded Autonomy: States and Industrial Transformation*, Princeton University Press, Princeton.

Evans, P.B., Rueschemeyer, D. and Skocpol, T. (eds) (1985), *Bringing the State Back In*, Cambridge University Press, Cambridge.

Finegold, K. and Skocpol, T. (1995), *State and Party in American's New Deal*, The University of Wisconsin Press, Wisconsin.

Fraser, D. (1984), *The Evolution of the British Welfare State*, Macmillan, London.

Giddens, A. (1971), *Capitalism and Modern Social Theory*, Cambridge University Press, Cambridge.

Giddens, A. (1984), *The Constitution of Society*, Polity Press, Cambridge.

Giddens, A. (1995), *Sociology*, Polity Press, Cambridge.

Giddens, A. (1998), *The Third Way: The Renewal of Social Democracy*, Policy Press, Cambridge.

Gilbert, N. (ed.) (1993), *Researching Social Life*, Sage, London.

Ginsburg, N. (1992), *Division of Welfare: A Critical Introduction to Comparative Social Policy*, Sage, London.

Glendinning, C. and Millar, J. (1992), *Women and Poverty in Britain: The 1990s*, Harvester Wheatsheaf, London.

Glennerster, H. (1995), *British Social Policy Since 1945*, Blackwell, Oxford.

Greenaway, J., Smith, S. and Street, J. (1992), *Deciding Factors in British Politics: A Case-Studies Approach*, Routledge, London.

Habermas, J. (1973), *Legitimation Crisis*, Heinemann, London.

Habermas, J. (1992), 'Citizenship and National Identity: Some Reflections on the Future of Europe', in Turner, B.S. and Hamilton, P. (eds) (1994), *Citizenship: Critical Concepts*, Routledge, London.

Hakim, C. (1995), 'Five Feminist Myths about Women's Employment', *British Journal of Sociology*, vol. 46, no. 3.

Hall, P., Land, H., Parker, R. and Webb, A. (1975), *Change, Choice and Conflict in Social Policy*, Heinemann, London.

Ham, C. and Hill, M. (1984), *The Policy Process in the Modern Capitalist State*,

Harvester Wheatsheaf, New York and London.

Ham, C. and Hill, M. (1993), *The Policy Process in the Modern Capitalist State*, Second Edition, Harvester Wheatsheaf, New York and London.

Healy, K. (1998) 'Conceptualizing Constraint: Mouzelis, Archer and the Concept of Social Structure', *Sociology*, vol. 32, no. 3, pp. 509-522.

Held, D. (1995a), *Political Theory and the Modern State*, Polity Press, Cambridge.

Held, D. (1995b), *Democracy and the Global Order*, Polity Press, Cambridge.

Held, D and Thompson, J. B. (eds) (1989), *Social Theory of Modern Societies: Anthony Giddens and His Critics*, Cambridge University Press, Cambridge.

Hennessy, P. (1996), *The Hidden Wiring: Unearthing the British Constitution*, Indigo, London.

Hernes, H.M. (1984), 'The Transition from Private to Public Dependence', in Holter, H. (ed.), *Patriarchy in a Welfare State*, Universitetsofrlaget, Oslo.

Hernes, H.M. (1988), 'The Welfare State Citizenship of Scandinavian Women', in Jones and Jonasdottir (eds), *The Political Interests of Gender*, Sage, London.

Hill, D.M. (1994), *Citizenship and Cities: Policy in the 1990s*, Harvester Wheatsheaf, London.

Hill, M. (ed.) (1993), *The Policy Process: A Reader*, Harvester Wheatsheaf, London.

Hill, M. (1997), *The Policy Process in the Modern State*, Third Edition, Harvester Wheatsheaf, London.

Hogwood, B. and Gunn, L. (1984), *Policy Analysis for the Real World*, Oxford University Press, Oxford.

House of Commons (HC), Session 1988-89, Paper no. 30-I, *Educational Provision for the Under-Fives*, HMSO, London.

HC, Session 1988-89, Education, Science and Arts Committee, *First Special Report*, 19 April 1989, HMSO, London.

HC, Session 1995-96, *Minutes of Proceedings on the Nursery Education and Grant-Maintained Schools Bill*, HC Paper no. 278, HMSO, London.

HC, Session 1996-97, Education and Employment Committee, Third Report, *The Operation of the Nursery Education Voucher Scheme*, March 1997, HMSO, London.

Jenkins, W.I. (1978), *Policy Analysis*, Martin Robertson, Oxford.

Jessop, B. (1985), *Nicos Poulantzas: Marxist Theory and Political Strategy*, Macmillan, London.

Jessop, B. (1990), *State Theory: Putting Capitalist States in their Place*, Polity Press, Cambridge.

Jewson, N. (1994), 'Family Values and Relationships', *Sociology Review*, February 1994.

Jordan, G. (1993), 'The New Right and Public Policy: a Preliminary Overview', in Jordan, G. and Ashford, N. (eds), *Public Policy and the Impact of the New Right*.

Jordan, G. and Ashford, N. (eds) (1993), *Public Policy and the Impact of the New Right*, Pinter Publishers, London.

Jordan, G. and Richardson, J. (1987), *British Politics and the Policy Process*, Allen and Unwin, London.

King, D. and Stoker, G. (eds) (1996), *Rethinking Local Democracy*, Macmillan, London.

Kingdon, J. (1984), *Agendas, Alternatives and Public Policies*, Little Brown and Co., Boston.

Knoke, D. (1990), *Political Networks: The Structural Perspective*, Cambridge University Press, Cambridge.

Kröger, T. (1997), 'The Dilemma of Municipalities: Scandinavian Approaches to Child Daycare Provision', *Journal of Social Policy*, vol. 26, no. 4, pp. 405-507.

Lewis, J. (1993), 'Introduction: Women, Work, Family and Social Policies in Europe', in Lewis (ed.), *Women and Social Policies in Europe*, Edward Elgar, Aldershot.

Lister, R. (1990), 'Women, Economic Dependency and Citizenship', in Turner, B.S. and Hamilton, P. (eds).

Lister, R. (1993), 'Tracing the Contours of Women's Citizenship', in *Policy and Politics*, vol. 21, no. 1., pp. 3-16.

Lister, R. (1997), *Citizenship: Feminist Perspectives*, Macmillan, London.

Liu, S. (2000a), *The Autonomous State of Childcare: Policy and the Policy Process in the UK*, unpublished Ph.D. thesis, University of Essex.

Liu, S. (2000b), 'Striving for Change: Childcare Policy in a Historical Context', paper presented at the British Sociological Association Annual Conference.

Liu, S (2000c), 'Structuration Theory and Deciding Factors in Policy Making: the Case of Childcare in Britain', *The Essex Graduate Journal of Sociology*, no. 3, pp. 15-30.

Local Government Management Board (LGMB) (1997), *Innovations in Public Participation*, LGMB, London.

Lockwood, D. (1956), 'Social Integration and System Integration', in Lockwood (1992), *Solidarity and Schism*, Clarendon, Oxford.

Lovenduski, J. and Randall, V. (1993), *Contemporary Feminist Politics: Women and Power in Britain*, Oxford University Press, Oxford.

Lukes, S. (1974), *Power: A Radical View*, Macmillan, London.

Lupton, C., Peckham, S. and Taylor, P. (1998), *Managing Public Involvement in Healthcare Purchasing*, Open University Press, Buckingham.

Maclean, M. and Groves, D. (1991), *Women's Issues in Social Policy*, Routledge, London.

Maltby, T. (1994), *Women and Pensions in Britain and Hungary*, Avebury, Aldershot.

Marchbank, J. (1996), 'The Political Mobilization of Women's Interest Issues: The Failure of Childcare', *Politics*, vol. 16, no. 1, pp. 9-15.

Marsh, D. (1995), 'State Theory and the Policy Network Model', Strathclyde Papers on Governments and Politics, no. 102, University of Strathclyde.

Marsh, D. and Rhodes, R.A.W. (eds) (1992), *Policy Networks in British Government*, Clarendon Press, Oxford.

Marshall, G. (ed.) (1994), *The Concise Oxford Dictionary of Sociology*, Oxford University Press, Oxford.

Marshall, T.H. (1964), *Class, Citizenship and Social Development*, Doubleday and

Company, New York.

Mazmanian, D.A. and Sabatier, P.A. (eds) (1981), *Effective Policy Implementation*, Lexington Books, Lexington.

McIntosh, M. (1978), 'The State and the Oppression of Women', in Kuhn *et al.* (eds) (1978), *Feminism and Materialism*, Routledge, London.

McIver, S. and Skelcher, C. (1997), *Consumerism and User Involvement in Public Services*, Occasional Paper 6, School of Public Policy, The University of Birmingham, Birmingham.

McLennan, G. 'Capitalist state or democratic polity? Recent developments in Marxist and pluralist theory', in McLennan, G. *et al.* (eds) (1984), *The Idea of the Modern State*.

McLennan, G. (1995), *Pluralism*, Open University Press, Buckingham.

McLennan, G., Held, D. and Hall, S. (eds) (1984), *The Idea of the Modern State*, Open University Press, Milton Keynes.

Meltzer, H. (1994), *Day care services for children: A survey carried out on behalf of the Department of Health in 1990*, HMSO, London.

Miliband, R. (1969), *The State in Capitalist Society*, Weidenfeld and Nicolson, London.

Morris, R. (1996), *The Nursery Education and Grant-Maintained Schools Bill: A critical commentary on the Bill and its second reading*, AMA, London.

Moss, P. (1991), 'Day care for young children in the United Kingdom', in Melhuish, E. C. and Moss, P. (eds), *Day Care for Young Children: International Perspectives*, Tavistock/Routledge, London and New York.

Mottershead, P. (1988), *Recent Developments in Childcare: A Review*, Equal Opportunities Commission Research Series, HMSO, Manchester.

Mouffe, C. (1993), *The Return of the Political*, Verso, London.

Mouzelis, N. (1995), *Sociological Theory: What Went Wrong?*, Routledge, London and New York.

Mullard, M. (1995), *Policy-making in Britain: An Introduction*, Routledge, London and New York.

National Early Years Network (NEYN) (1997), *Choosing What's Best for Your Child: A Guide to Education for Four-Year-Olds*, NEYN, London.

National Children's Bureau (NCB), Early Childhood Unit (1998), *Learning from Vouchers: An Evaluation of Phase One of the Four Year Old Voucher Scheme 1996/7*, in press, NCB, London.

Nordlinger, E.A. (1981), *On the Autonomy of the Democratic State*, Harvard University Press, Massachusetts.

O'Brien, M. and Dench, S. (1996), *The Out-of-School Childcare Grant Initiative: A Second Evaluation*, HMSO, London.

Office for National Statistics (1998), *Social Focus on Women and Men*, HMSO, London.

Office of the Minister for the Civil Service (1989), *Career Break and Childcare Provisions in the Civil Service*, HMSO, London.

Okin, S.M. (1989), *Justice, Gender, and the Family*, Basic Books, New York.

Palmer, J. (1991), *Childcare in Rural Communities: Scotland in Europe - Scottish Child and Family Alliance*, HMSO, Edinburgh.

Parkin, F. (1972), 'System Contradiction and Political Transformation', in Giddens and Held (eds) (1982), *Class, Power and Conflict*, Macmillan, London.

Parsons, T. (1965), 'Full Citizenship for the Negro American: A Sociological Problem', in Turner and Hamilton (eds).

Pascall, G. (1986), *Social Policy: a Feminist Analysis*, Tavistock Publications, London and New York.

Pateman, C. (1989), *The Disorder of Women: Democracy, Feminism and Political Theory*, Polity Press, Cambridge.

Petrie, P. (1994), *Play and Care Out of School*, HMSO, London.

Petrie, P. and Logan, P. (1986), *After school and in the Holidays*, Thomas Coram Research Unit, Working Papers 2, Thomas Coram Research Centre, London.

Phillips, A. (1993), *Democracy and Difference*, Polity Press, Cambridge.

Platt, J. (1981), 'Evidence and proof in documentary research', *Sociological Review*, vol. 29, no. 1, pp. 31-66.

Poulantzas, N. (1973), *Political Power and Social Class*, New Left Books, London.

Poulantzas, N. (1978), *State, Power, Socialism*, Verso, London.

Pre-school Learning Alliance (PLA) (1995), *Pre-school Learning Alliance Annual Review*, PLA, London.

PLA (1996a), *Nursery Vouchers: What Do They Mean for Your Pre-school*, PLA, London.

PLA (1996b), *Nursery Education Voucher Initiative: Briefing for Sub-committees*, PLA, London.

PLA (1996c), *Nursery Vouchers: Preparing for Inspection*, PLA, London.

Pringle, R. and Sophie W. (1992), 'Women's Interests and the Post-Structuralist State', in Barrett and Phillips (eds) (1992), *Destabilizing Theory: Contemporary Feminist Debates*, Polity, Cambridge.

Pugh, G. (1996), 'A Policy for Early Childhood Services?', in Pugh, G (ed.), *Contemporary issues in the Early Years*, second edition, PCP in association with the NCB, London.

Pyper, R. and Robins, L. (eds) (1995), *Governing the UK in the 1990s*, St. Martin's Press, New York.

Randall, V. (1994), 'The Politics of Child Daycare: Some European Comparisons', in *Frauen und Politik*, Schweizerisches Jahrbuch För Politische Wissenschaften 34/1994, pp. 165-177.

Randall, V. (1995), 'The Irresponsible State? The Politics of Child Daycare Provision in Britain', *British Journal of Political Science*, vol. 25, pp. 327-348.

Randall, V. (1996), 'The Politics of Child Care Policy', *Parliamentary Affairs*, vol. 49, no. 1, pp. 176-190.

Randall, V. (1996), 'Feminism and Child Daycare', *Journal of Social Policy*, vol. 25, no. 4.

Rhodes, R.A.W. (1986), *The National World of Local Government*, Allen and Unwin, London.

Rhodes, R.A.W. (1988), *Beyond Westminster and Whitehall: The Sub-Central Governments of Britain*, Unwin Hyman, London.

Rhodes, R.A.W. (1997), *Understanding Governance: Policy Networks, Governance, Reflexivity and Accountability*, Open University Press, Buckingham.

Richardson, D. (1998), 'Sexuality and Citizenship', *Sociology*, vol. 32, no. 1, pp. 83-100.

Richardson, J.J. and Jordan, A.G. (1979), *Governing Under Pressure*, Martin Robertson, Oxford.

Ruggie, M. (1984), *The State and Working Women: A Comparative Study of Britain and Sweden*, Princeton University Press, Princeton.

Sainsbury, D. (ed.) (1994), *Gendering Welfare States*, Sage, London.

Sainsbury, D. (1994), 'Women's and Men's Social Rights: Gendering Dimensions of Welfare States', in Sainsbury, D. (ed.).

Sanderson, I. *et al.* (1995), *The Out-of-school Childcare Grant Initiative: An Interim Evaluation*, Department of Employment, London.

Savage, S.P., Atkinson, R. and Robins, L. (eds) (1994), *Public Policy in Britain*, St. Martin's Press, New York.

Scott, Joan (1988), *Gender and the Politics of History*, Columbia University Press, Columbia.

Scott, John (1990), *A Matter of Record*, Polity Press, Cambridge.

Scott, John (1995), *Sociological Theory*, Edward Elgar, Hants.

Shanley, M.L. and Pateman, C. (eds) (1991), *Feminist Interpretations and Political Theory*, Polity Press, Cambridge.

Siim, B. (1988), 'Towards a Feminist Rethinking of the Welfare State', in Jones and Jonasdottir (eds).

Siim, B. (1995), 'New Dilemmas in the Theory and Practice of Women's Citizenship', paper presented at the Second European Sociological Association Conference.

Skocpol, T. (1985), 'Bring the State Back In: Strategies of Analysis in Current Research', in Evans, P.B., *et al.* (eds).

Skocpol, T. (1992), *Protecting Soldiers and Mothers: The Political Origins of Social Policy in the United States*, The Belknap Press of Harvard University Press, Cambridge.

Sly, F., Price, A. and Risdon, A., 'Women in the Labour Market: Results from the Spring 1996 Labour Force Survey', *Labour Market Trends*, March 1996, HMSO, London.

Smith, M. (1999), *Evaluating Community Involvement: Tools and Techniques for Multi Sector Partnerships*, Occasional Paper 24, School of Public Policy, The University of Birmingham, Birmingham.

Smith, M.J. (1990), *The Politics of Agricultural Support in Britain*, Dartmouth, Hants.

Smith, M.J. (1993), *Pressure, Power and Policy*, Harvester Wheatsheaf, London.

Smith, M.J. (1999), *The Core Executive in Britain*, Macmillan, London.

Sonya, M. (1999), *Children's Interests/Mothers' Rights: the Shaping of America's Child Care Policy*, Yale University Press, New Haven.

Stewart, J. and Stoker, G. (eds) (1995), *Local Government in the 1990s*, Macmillan, London.

Stones, R. (1988), *The Myth of Betrayal: Structure and Agency in the Labour Government's Policy of Non-devaluation 1964-67*, unpublished Ph.D. thesis, University of Essex.

Stones, R. (1990), 'Government-Finance Relations in Britain 1964-7: a Tale of Three Cities', *Economy and Society*, vol. 19, no. 1, pp. 32-55.

Thair, T. and Risdon, A. (1999), 'Women in the Labour Market: Results from the Spring 1998 Labour Force Survey', *Labour Market Trends*, March 1999, Office for National Statistics, HMSO, London.

Turner, B.S. (1990), 'Outline of a Theory of Citizenship', in Turner, B.S. and Hamilton, P. (eds).

Turner, B.S. (1993), 'Outline of a Theory of Human Rights', in Turner, B.S. and Hamilton, P. (eds).

Turner, B.S. and Hamilton, P. (eds) (1994), *Citizenship: Critical Concepts*, Routledge, London.

Ungerson, C. (ed.) (1985), *Women and Social Policy: A Reader*, Macmillan, London.

Unison, *Inside the Voucher Scheme: the Impact of Nursery Education Vouchers upon Unison Members and the Services they Provide to Children under Five*, September 1996, London.

Walby, S. (1990), *Theorizing Patriarchy*, Blackwell, Oxford.

Walt, G. (1994), *Health Policy: An Introduction to Process and Power*, Witwatersrand University Press, Johannesburg, and Zed Books, London and New Jersey.

Ward, C., Dale, A. and Joshi, H. (1996), 'Combining Employment with Childcare: An Escape from Dependence?', *Journal of Social Policy*, vol. 25, no. 2, pp. 223-247.

White, R., Carr, P. and Lowe, N. (1990), *A Guide to the Children Act 1989*, Butterworths, London.

Williams, F. (1989), *Social Policy: A Critical Introduction*, Polity Press, Cambridge.

Wilson, D. (1995), 'Elected Local Government and Central-Local Relations', in Pyper, R. and Robins, L. (eds), *Governing the UK in the 1990s*, St. Martin's Press, New York.

Wright, R. (1994), *Policy Networks Analysis: Theories and Applications*, unpublished draft paper.

Young, I.M. (1989), 'Polity and Group Difference: A Critique of the Ideal of Universal Citizenship', in Turner, B.S. and Hamilton, P. (eds).

Young, I.M. (1990), *Justice and the Politics of Difference*, Princeton University Press, Princeton.

Younis, T. (ed.) (1990), *Implementation in Public Policy*, Dartmouth, Aldershot.

Newspapers and Journals

Childcare News
Childcare Now, Daycare Trust, London.

Community Care
Co-ordinate
Education
Hansard
Nursery World
Official Report, House of Lords, London.
The Daily Mail
The Daily Mirror
The Guardian
The Independent
The Independent on Sunday
The Sunday Telegraph
The Sunday Times
The Telegraph
The Times
The Times Educational Supplement (TES)
Term Time
Under Five Contact, PLA, London.
Who Minds?, NCMA, London.

Index